The
Scorecard

The Scorecard

The Official Point System for Keeping
Score in the Relationship Game

Greg Gutfeld

BARNES
&NOBLE
BOOKS
NEW YORK

To my mother: for drinking, smoking, and having a good time while pregnant with me. It seems to have paid off.

Contents

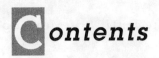

Contents

THE
SCORECARD

Introduction

Walk into any bookstore and you will be beseiged by hundreds—no, *thousands*—of relationship books claiming to possess the answer to your marital or relationship woes. And for $21.95 and future access to your credit card number, that answer is yours.

Millions of these books are sold every year. But more important than the sheer numbers is this simple point: nearly all of these books are read by women. Old women, young women, middle-aged women, women in love, women in prison, women in love with prisoners. And then there's former cast members of "Facts of Life," which accounts for 30 percent of all purchases.

The reason for this is simple: Relationships are to women what football is to men. Women like to read about relationships, talk about relationships, dissect relationships, even root for and against them. They argue over trick plays and strategies, and on occasion, offer their insights to close friends once they have proven successful. And just as in football, women also wear protective padding when necessary.

Men, however, treat relationships in a far more simple and straightforward manner. We give up. We surrender. We acknowledge freely that we know nothing of the pink and paisley world of romance. Instead, we adhere to only one basic rule.

Make her happy.

Did you get that? Here, I'll repeat it: Make her happy.

Bring her happiness—pure and simple—your life is transformed. Your career moves swimmingly as promotion after promotion rolls your way. Your abdominal muscles will ripple to the surface like anatomical speed bumps, with little, if any, effort on your part. Even better, you will cultivate a mane of wild blond hair that will dance playfully over your well muscled, tattooed shoulders. And you'll get cable television without paying, too.

Yes, make her happy, and she will always find you sexually irresistible, even when you've all but neglected the basic tenets of personal hygiene. To use a baseball metaphor you can easily grasp, life becomes a succulent parade of hanging curveballs, and you're a Louisville Slugger.

With this simple rule in mind, an intelligent man realizes that in order to preserve his happiness, he must guarantee his mate's as well. In the spirit of love, sex, peace, and under the threat of potential bank-draining alimony payments, he must make deals and trade-offs to keep himself forever in her good graces. It is this such strategy that will keep him forever out of the doghouse. Got that?

....

THE RISE OF THE SCORECARD . . . AND THE FALL OF THE DOGHOUSE

There are problems, however. We never know if we're in the doghouse, and once we are in it, we can't find the way out. In the process of becoming civilized, we have become confused. It is as though we are playing a board game and our opponent is a maniacal Parker Brother.

What we need is a simple method to help us understand how women think about men. We need a decoder of sorts, to let us know when she is happy with us, and when she's upset enough to banish us to the fold-out for the night. Even more, what we really need are objective measurements to help us translate our partner's emotional reactions into something we can understand. Numbers, man. We need numbers.

You got it. What you have in your hands is The Scorecard, the first and only scorekeeping system that tallies up your good deeds and your bad, and attributes to them actual point value. This will function as a handy little checklist that—at any juncture in your relationship—gives you an idea of where you stand in her eyes (even when you're on your knees begging for forgiveness). It can also double as a pillow for those nights on the couch.

We will reveal to you the true secrets of the relationship game. We will lay bare the mode of assessment women have employed for generations as they grade our effort to be worthy partners. You will finally learn why you've spent so much time in the doghouse, and better, how never to get thrown in there again.

Mind you, this novel little enterprise was not developed on a napkin in the cellar of a smoky bar in Emmaus, Pennsylvania (although you're pretty damn close). This elaborate system had to be flawlessly designed. So we contacted renowned physicist Stephen Hawking. When he refused to return our calls, we decided to seek out more reliable advice: our married brethren and coworkers, those ragtag survivors of long-term monogamy, and asked them how they've negotiated the stormy seas of romance.

And we devised a simple method to gauge the rewards for your noble efforts (such as taking out the trash) and weigh them against the damage incurred from your really moronic moves (such as cheating at Monopoly). And when you do something really, really stupid (such as investing in string art), this point system can accurately predict how long it will be before you're sharing a damp refrigerator box and fighting over pizza crust with a colony of fattened rodents out behind the local bowling alley.

HOW THE SCORECARD OPERATES

Like everything in life (or everything that costs $9.95 and promises eternal happiness and sex at regular intervals), The Scorecard comes with a set of rules and regulations. We know these rules can be unfair. But hey, it's not like we invented them . . .

1. You get absolutely no points by simply meeting her expectations.

There are some things that are expected of you. Examples of important but "pointless" duties include: reminding her that you love her, not sleeping with her sister, maintaining your original gender throughout the relationship, always buying her flowers on her birthday, paying for expensive dinners (even on *your* birthday), and not taking an airliner hostage (especially around the holidays). While we applaud you for meeting these requirements, don't expect points for them. Do them and do not complain. No one is listening. Especially her.

2. Getting points has a larger purpose than you think.

Acquiring points not only keeps you out of trouble and elevates your position in the relationship, it also helps you plan ahead.

Do good deeds and you rack up points—creating a handy reservoir to draw from when you need it most. Example: Enough points might allow you to see the Bulls with your pals, even when the last Lamaze class falls on the same night. Soon you can earn points for really big things in life, like purchasing an oversized camper, a big screen television, or a Flobee hair trimmer.

3. Good deeds, and the points earned, have a short shelf life.

Sincere acts of consideration will earn you points. But you need to realize they all have a shelf life. In order for these points to be traded for, say, free unsupervised time with your unstable single friends, you must do your good deed within a day (that's twenty-four hours) of the anticipated reward. Example: You want to watch the Celtics on TV tonight? Clean the garage this morning. You want to see the game in person? Clean the garage and paint the exterior, that same day. If you don't, she won't make the connection, and all that effort is wasted. It would be no different than working hard, making a ton of money, and investing it in solar power.

4. But a bad deed can last forever (or at least three weeks).

While good deeds have a short shelf life, bad deeds can linger on like a Fox sitcom for months—even years. Women have a way of remembering every bad thing you do, down to the most humiliating detail. Whether or not you recall that stolen moment in fall of 1993 at the No Finer Diner when you glanced down the tube top of the sixteen-year-old cashier is of no one's concern. The fact that your mate remembers it—down to the shade of lip gloss this lass had smeared across her face—is all that matters now. And the longer your mate holds a bad deed over your head, the more she can extract from you. You're like a stock portfolio of reliable services. As long as you're in the doghouse, you pay dividends. This is why you should avoid committing any major blunders—i.e., acts of marital infidelity, developing a coke habit, burning down the house, or accidentally shooting the cat with a speargun.

5. Saturday and Sunday are gold mines.

Weekends provide the best opportunity to gain the most points. By undertaking a massive home-improvement project (painting the house, carpeting the basement, moving Gramps into or out of the attic), you'll be paid with a lump sum of points, to be used for such endeavors as a camping trip with your pals, a poker night in the den, one free pass to escape the in-laws. Embrace these big projects, for they will become your ticket to temporary freedom. And they also give you the excuse to drink beer before noon.

6. Your mate is not stupid.

Don't expect to negotiate over unreasonable requests. No matter how many times you take her shopping for expensive beveled wind chimes, you will never get the green light to play naked Twister with your fetching new secretary. The transaction must be reasonable, which essentially means you should be happy with whatever you get.

....

YOUR SCORECARD

Before you read any further, grab a pencil. You'll need it to tally up your score. Of course, that score will mean nothing without some expert interpretation. Below is a handy chart that helps you figure out where you stand once you've calculated all your plusses and minuses.

First, however, we must take into account the *The Lie Factor*. We realize that as you work your way through The Scorecard and start keeping score of your own actions, you will be faced with an uncontrollable urge to fudge. But the sad truth is, cheating only makes matters worse. By not scoring honestly, you'll never know where you stand, for real, in your relationship with her. In the end it will come back and sting you with serious doghouse time. One day you will come home from work expecting a nice hot meal, a cool drink and a quick roll in the hay. Instead you will find her standing in the driveway with a sawed-off shotgun, arm in arm with her new boyfriend—a bloated, disoriented Mickey Rourke.

So use The Scorecard honestly. And you may not end up living alone in a trailer park wearing sweaters made of old newspapers. Unless, of course, that has always been your dream. Then we're behind you 100 percent.

YOUR GUIDE TO THE DOGHOUSE

+1000 points. You have mastered the game. You are not only miles beyond ever setting foot in the doghouse, she is actually in *your* doghouse! Of course, you're about as likely to reach that milestone as you are to break Cal Ripken's consecutive-game streak.

+500 points. Good work. Keep this bank account up, and you'll have more freedoms than mortal men like us even dream of. For example, you can barbecue at will. Think about that when you're changing the lightbulbs of her vanity mirror.

+250 points. You should be proud. She's happy. You're happy. And you haven't broken anything expensive in the process. Now have a beer already. And get back to the vanity mirror.

+100 points. Not bad. Your head is above water, you're dog paddling to safety. But remember, one big and bad false move could put you back in the doghouse without supper.

0 points. You're flat-lining. Sounds bad, but frankly that's where most of us are. All that really means is that your status fluctuates daily, depending on the little things you do. Our advice: start cleaning more, drinking less.

−100 points. You're in a bad spot, but not a hopeless one. Think about throwing the long ball. Ever consider buying her a mink? (And we mean a coat.)

−250 points. Dire straits, buddy, and we aren't talking music. Time to make some major long-term changes. Do you still have buddies living in Thailand?

−500 points. You are in deep, deep trouble, friend. To get out of the doghouse, you're going to have to hand her your cojones on a pastel-colored plate. Or at least buy her a minivan. A *magenta* minivan.

−1000 points. Congratulations. You have plummeted to the depths of the doghouse. Have you ever considered writing a book?

1 THE EARLY YEARS

MAKING A FIRST IMPRESSION

You're elbow to elbow at your local watering hole. You don't know her. She doesn't know you. And the moment you open your mouth, she's judging you. If you want to lose points fast, just:

- tell her she looks like someone famous **–3**
- like, say, Meryl Streep **–6**
- or, say, Merle Haggard **–500**
- tell her you've been told you look like someone famous **–5**
- like, say, George Clooney **–10**
- and you look like George Costanza **–35**

Complain about being burdened with "a gift"

- like, say, tremendous wealth **–10**
- or academic brilliance **–12**
- or genital size **–15**

- yell "Party!" **–25**
- yell "Fire!" **–125**

- say "What you need is a shot." **–15**
- say "What you need is a back rub." **–20**
- say, "What you need is a nose job." **–30**

- introduce yourself, followed by your job title **–15**
- introduce yourself, followed by the make of your car **–16**
- brag about your humidor **–17**
- show her your scars **–47**

- espouse your political views, left or right **–17**
- defend the artistic talents of Adam Sandler **–34**

- go off on conspiracy tangents **–20**
- try to make her frightened of her tap water **–30**
- ask her if she has ever been abducted by aliens **–50**
- forget to remove the name tag from your most recent Star Trek convention **–75**

- say, "I think I can take him" **–15**
- while referring to the elderly man in a wheelchair **–50**

- say, "You'd be great in my movie" **–14**
- then outlining her face with your hands as though you were picturing her on film **–40**

- brag that you knew Billy Idol before he was famous **–20**
- brag that you are Billy Idol **–30**

- mention that you can get backstage passes to something cool **+3**
- then when she calls you on it, change the subject **–45**

- get to know her really well, make her laugh and act charming **+5**
- until the waiter comes around for drink orders, and then you slink back into the darkness **–60**

- talk like Oprah ("Go, girl!") **–34**
- dress like Oprah **–478**

- make sure she can see your labels **–20**
- even though you buy your stuff at Chess King **–80**

···

NEXT STOP: YOU'VE GAINED ENTRY

It looks like you've made contact. Just remember, she's still tallying up your score.

- You're at the bar, you make eye contact, and, in time, she returns your glance. **+2**
- When she returns your glance, you offer to buy her a drink. **+4**
- When she returns your glance, you wave your car keys. **–50**
- They're from an AMC Pacer **–75**

- When you approach her, you say something simple and genuine, like, "I just wanted to say hello and see if I might treat you to a drink." **0**

- When you approach her, you say, "Here let me clean off a place so you can sit down" and run your hand across your face. **−30**

- You ask her what she does for a living, and she tells you she's a court reporter. **0**
- You say, "Great, I love basketball!" **−4**

- She asks you what you do for a living, and you tell her you're a fireman. **+10**
- You sell insurance. **−5**
- She knows you sell insurance because you forgot to remove your nametag that reads: "Hi, my name is Vic and I sell insurance." **−23**

- You offer to buy a her a drink. **+4**
- You offer to buy her a house. **−130**

- At the end of the night, you accompany her to her car. **+5**
- You ask her for her phone number and she gives it to you. **+8**
- You write it down on your hand and joke, "I won't wash this off until I see you." **+2**
- You write it beneath three other numbers. **−15**
- Belonging to her friends. **−60**

- As you say good-bye, you shake her hand and give her a hug. **+3**
- You give a nice peck on the cheek. **+2**
- You attempt a sloppy tongue kiss. **−12**
- She turns her head away **−35**
- so she can mace you. **−89**

THE FIRST DATE

- You arrive at the restaurant, dressed like a million bucks. **+10**
- You even pressed your khakis. **+1**
- And your Lynyrd Skynryd tour T-shirt looks smashing. **−23**

- You take her to a fine restaurant where you are well known by the staff **+15**
- as a bad tipper **−20**
- which is why you're seated under the air duct that sounds like a jet engine. **−30**

- When ordering food, she orders hummus and black beans and you still don't figure out she's a vegetarian. **−8**
- You order the all-you-can-eat rib special **−5**
- and make a fort out of the bones. **−54**

- When the meal is over, you unbutton your pants and pat your belly. **−15**
- You unbutton her pants and pat her belly. **−30**

- During dinner, you impress her with tales of your exciting job and frequent jaunts across the globe. **+13**
- You casually mention how your stock options have allowed you the financial freedom most guys your age can't even imagine. **+15**
- When the bill arrives, you pick it up, inspect it, and say, "Okay, let's see . . . I only had the shrimp scampi but you had an appetizer and . . ." **−80**

- After dinner, you move to a dark corner of the bar, so you can enjoy a drink together. **+4**

- After dinner, you move to the dark corner of the bar so no one will recognize you. −15
- Especially your wife. −175

- On the drive home, you engage in more conversation, mostly about world peace. +5
- On the drive home, you're already removing your socks. −10

- As you walk toward your building, you put your arm around her. +6
- And you mention you've got a great view of the city on your roof. +8
- Actually, it's the roof of your parents' house. −8
- You live in their attic. −34
- Nice love beads. −70

MODE OF TRANSPORTATION:

Sometimes, it's not who you are, but how you got to her apartment.

- Volvo station wagon with its high safety rating +35
- BMW roadster with a convertible top. +30
- a used pickup truck −5
- your dad's 1977 Cutlass Supreme, −20
- which smells like Vicks −22
- public transit −100
- an old Schwinn with a well-worn banana seat −125
- your thumb −200

....

THE TELL-TALE DATE

There are dates, and then there are dates. The most important date: the one that *starts* at your apartment. And ends there, too. Just be aware that, at this point, a woman has her mental abacus at high rev, constantly rating your value as matrimonial material. And once she is at your apartment, she has a golden opportunity to see how you really are: in your habitat, your cage, your little piece of hell. And because you've already been putting up a nice facade, you've driven her to be even more diligent with her detective work.

PREPARATION

- Before she arrives at your apartment, you tidy up. **+3**
- You hide the adult videos, the girlie magazines, and the pictures of your ex in a big box in the closet. **+6**
- But you forget to take down the bondage cage. **−15**

- You actually change your sheets and make the bed. **+6**
- And you tell her so, repeatedly, throughout dinner. **−34**

- You scrub the toilet **+3**
- clean the bathroom sink **+5**
- wash down the countertops **+4**
- comb your hair **+3**
- all with the same brush. **−10**

- You inspect your medicine cabinet, and remove anything that might be incriminating **+4**

- like the hemorrhoidal cream and your collection of glow-in-the-dark condoms. **+10**
- You replace those items with stuff you hope will impress her if she bothers snooping, **+4**
- like herbal extracts and "not-tested-on-animals" natural shaving cream. **+6**
- She still manages to zero in on the tubes of Herpecin. **−12**

- You move from room to room, removing anything that hints of slovenly behavior **+6**
- like dirty underwear, pizza boxes, beer bottles, and dog-eared *TV Guides* **+3**
- You replace these things with items she might find more appealing **+7**
- like topiaries, an acoustic guitar, books by John Bradshaw and a small puppy. **+15**
- You still manage to light the candles from a matchbook advertising "970-BUNS." **−25**

- You hang up one of those framed, artsy black-and-white posters of a man and woman kissing passionately in front of a train. **+5**
- You forget to take down your "Stacked and Packed" calendar. **−34**

- Before she arrives, you put on a CD, preferably something mellow and romantic:
- Luther Vandross **+3**
- Lou Rawls **+4**
- Harry Connick, Jr. **+5**
- "Jock Rock," vol. 1 **−24**
- Anything by John Tesh **−150**

SHE ARRIVES

- You greet her at the door, take her jacket, and give her an innocent peck on the cheek. **+2**
- You greet her at the door with wildflowers, take her jacket, and give her an innocent peck on the cheek. **+4**
- You greet her at the door in your bathrobe **−15**
- and you've got a camcorder rolling. **−60**

- You offer her a glass of wine, an award-winning Merlot from a top Napa vineyard. **+10**
- You offer her a can of beer, from a cooler by the television. **−15**

- You give her a tour of your apartment, **+15**
- you hustle her toward the bedroom. **−30**

- You offer your date a choice of hors d'oeuvres:
- hummus and pita bread **+3**
- fresh cut vegetables and nonfat sour cream dip **+5**
- Cheetos and Mr. Pibb **−24**

- You ask her about her day, showing sincere interest in her thoughts. **+15**
- as you try to pull her sweater over her head. **−70**

DINNER

- You enhance the meal with candles and soft music. **+30**
- You've convinced yourself she really doesn't mind eating Froot Loops from the box. **−24**

- For dessert you picked up slices of the city's finest cheesecake. **+13**

- For dessert, you show her the neat stuff you can do with Twizzlers. **−15**

- After dinner, when the two of you are relaxed, you suggest giving her a back rub. **+10**
- You begin rubbing her shoulders, and she moans softly and clearly enjoys it. **+15**
- Your parents come downstairs to tell you to keep it quiet. **−100**

SCORING MUSIC

Your CD collection says a lot about you as a person. Folk ballads hint at your sensitivity, Black Sabbath hints at your past involvement in animal sacrifice, and Kenny G. tells everyone about your stay at the local mental institution. Here's what to leave around the apartment, and what to hide under the bed.

MUSIC TO SCORE POINTS TO:

- Anything by Mary Chapin Carpenter **+10**
- Anything by Sting, or sounding remotely like Sting (think ferrets) **+10**
- Carole King's most famous album; which, of course, you should know the name of **+10**
- *Rent:* The Original Cast Album **+10**
- Any of Alanis Morissette's sonic bleatings **+10**
- Any rock benefit album, whatever the cause (the NRA being the exception) **+10**

- Canadian folk music collections from the early 1970s **+10**
- Anything by Tori Amos, Tracy Chapman, k.d. lang or Melissa Etheridge **+10**
- The Beatles White Album (you don't need that actual CD, the box will do fine) **+10**

MUSIC THAT WILL COST YOU

- Anything by Marilyn Manson, White Zombie, Slayer, Ministry, or Jesus Lizard **−12**
- Comedy albums **−23**
- Music featuring extended drum or guitar solos. **−19**
- Music that makes you want to pound your fist in the air **−21**
- or roll down your car window and "rock out" **−22**
- Music with liner notes that dedicate the album to Charles Manson or to "my homeys in Compton." **−24**
- The Butthole Surfers (the name alone costs you points) **−25**
- Respectful old people music (i.e., Eric Clapton, The Beach Boys) **−30**
- Any stuff you purchased as a kid that may cast a shadow on your character now (Styx, Kansas, ELO, Fleetwood Mac, Gerry Rafferty, Boz Scaggs, and anyone else you thought was cool when you used to be driven to school by your mom) **−67**

YOUR JOB

Status means everything. If you don't have a cool-sounding job, then lie, or go to night school.

- You're a highly paid executive. **+10**
- You're a highly paid lawyer. **+9**
- You're a highly paid test subject for a new experimental drug. **−34**
- Nice twitch. **−50**

- You're in the entertainment business **+12**
- meaning you're a character at Disneyland. **−20**

- You're a fireman. **+7**
- You're a cop. **+3**
- You're a cop who'll tear up her parking tickets. **+9**

- You're heavily into securities. **+15**
- You're a heavy security guard. **−20**

- You're an accountant. **−11**
- You're the Smashing Pumpkins' accountant. **+22**
- You're Siegfried and Roy's accountant. **−76**

- You're in a band. **+14**
- It's a famous rock band. **+100**
- It's an obscure wedding band **−14**
- known for its sensitive rendition of "Feelings." **−45**
- "Would you like to hear it?" **−70**

- You're in the stock market. **+50**
- You're a stock boy, at the market. **−50**

....

AS THE RELATIONSHIP GROWS

As you get to know her better, she only gets better at assessing your faults. She's got her "buyer's" face on, and she's more than willing to kick the tires (Note: that's a metaphor).

....

HER BIRTHDAY

- You buy her a gift **0**
- and it's a small appliance **−15**
- like an electric food dehydrator. **−25**
- You think it'll be great for parties. **−30**
- You lost the receipt. **−100**

- You buy her a gift, and it's not a small appliance. **+1**
- It's a box of chocolates you picked up at the drugstore. **−10**
- It was marked down 75 percent **−20**
- and you already ate two caramels on the way to her place. **−30**

- It's her birthday, and you actually plan ahead of time for this special event, with dinner reservations at an exclusive restaurant **+15**
- the kind that has valet parking **+5**

- the kind that has food on the menu you cannot pronounce +5
- and you try to pay with a two-for-one coupon. −40

- You hire a guitar player to get up and sing +10
- her favorite song +20
- your favorite song. −20
- It's the theme song from "The Jeffersons." −40

- You purchase an expensive gift, one you'll be paying off for months to come. +30
- It's a beautiful pearl necklace. +75
- It's a pair of diamond earrings. +100
- It's a remote control dune buggy that can do back flips on the carpet. −20

- You buy her something you think she might honestly have some use for, +6
- a case of SlimFast. −400

THE GIFTOMETER

When you give her:

- any kind of gift certificate −2
- a scarf −4
- scented bath soaps −8
- a tin of storebought cookies −10
- an inspirational plaque −15
- a bag of hard candy −20

- a bag of ribbon candy **–25**
- crotchless underwear **–30**
- a universal remote **–47**
- a universal remote shaped like a handgun **–48**
- a real handgun **–49**
- Vermont Teddy Bears **–55**

THE BIRTHDAY CARD

- You give her a greeting card with the standard, drippy, preprinted sentiment inside **–1**
- without adding any personal note. **–4**
- Someone else's name is erased at the bottom. **–45**

- There are coin slots in this greeting card. **–5**
- They are empty. **–6**

- When you give her the card, you scrawl your own personal message, expressing your love, below the standard, drippy, preprinted sentiment. **+15**
- She realizes you stole it from Dr. Seuss. **–6**

- You don't buy her a card but actually make one of your own. **+5**
- It's tastefully done with fine paper and a handwritten love poem inside. **+10**
- It's a limerick. **–15**
- The last word of the last line rhymes with Venus. **–40**

- You buy her a novelty card. **−4**
- The kind with obese naked people all over it. **−6**
- She opens it in front of her folks. **−15**
- They recognize Uncle Sal. **−45**

THOUGHTFULNESS

- You forget her birthday completely. −50
- You forget your anniversary. −75
- You forget to pick her up at the bus station −100
- which is in Newark, New Jersey −125
- and the rain dissolves her body cast. −200

HER EX-BOYFRIEND

Women feel that every new boyfriend should be an improvement over the last one. If she realizes you're a step backward, you will lose points faster than your hair.

- You and your mate run into her old boyfriend, who is a highly successful investment banker for a top brokerage firm in New York City. −3
- You're not nearly as successful as he is, so you try to make up for it by acting like an extremely successful person yourself +4
- which is hard to do when you're still wearing the clown outfit. −24

- You and your mate run into her old boyfriend, and you get along fine. +5

- You pair off to a corner at a party and start commiserating. **–5**
- Your mate comes over just as you say, "She did *that* on the third date?" **–44**

- You are introduced to her old beau, and you act very polite. **+2**
- You lie about your accomplishments. **–3**
- You tell him you work for the CIA. **–10**
- You're actually a CPA **–20**
- an unemployed CPA. **–25**
- He offers you a job. **–27**
- You accept **–35**
- as you tell yourself you'll really enjoy the prestige of driving his limousine. **–60**

- You meet the guy and talk to him about work, sports, the stock market. **+4**
- You mention how great sex has been lately with your mate. **–4**
- He agrees. **–10**

- You get him a beer and get along with him **–4**
- almost too well. **–8**
- You start taking him to parties instead of your mate. **–33**
- She finds both of you shopping for furniture at Ikea. **–50**

YOUR EX-GIRLFRIEND

Once you have become involved with a woman, the past means almost nothing to her. Except, of course, when it comes to old girlfriends.

- An old girlfriend calls you up, and you don't mention it to your mate. −**10**
- But your mate finds out anyway. −**15**
- Perhaps it was $300 worth of late night calls on the phone bill that gave it away. −**50**

- When she asks you about your old girlfriend, you reply, "Honey, as far as I am concerned, you were the first, and you will always be the best." +**5**
- When she asks about your old girlfriend, you reply, "Honey, there's only so much great sex a guy can take. I'm over that." −**25**
- You add, "Can you get me a beer?" −**75**

- When your old girlfriend calls, you tell your mate it's nothing to worry about +**2**
- and that's why you've invited your ex to stay for the weekend. −**90**

- When you and your mate disagree about something, you say, "You're right, I guess I never looked at it that way." +**5**
- When you and your mate disagree, you say, "Well, (*insert ex-girlfriend's name here*) never felt that way" −**34**
- You say this when asking her to dress up like Princess Leia. −**50**

- No one ever brings up your old flame in front of your current mate. +**3**
- Wherever you go with your mate, someone always asks you how (*insert old flame's name here*) is, and how come you're no longer a couple. −**16**

- "You always seemed so right together," says one. **−20**
- Actually, your mom said that. **−34**

- When you and your mate run into your old girlfriend, you wrap your arm tightly around your mate's waist. **+5**
- You whisper to your mate, "Boy, time hasn't been kind to her!" **+10**
- You whisper to your mate, "You ever think about getting implants?" **−24**

- You still have pictures of your ex. **−5**
- You hid them so your mate cannot find them. **0**
- She found them. **−20**
- They were in between the mattress and box spring. **−78**
- They were in the secret shrine, in the toolshed. **−190**

NAMES OF EX-GIRLFRIENDS

The more exotic the name, the more they cost you.

- Agnes **+5**
- Eunice **+5**
- Alexis **−2**
- Heather **−3**
- Jade **−7**
- Ursula **−8**
- Uma **−18**
- Iman **−20**
- Inmate 324641 LGF **−65**

···

DEALING WITH HER CAT

Men, by nature, hate cats, and if society would only permit it, we would gladly make cool jackets and jerky out of them. But sadly, felines hold a special place in the hearts and minds of women, and it is in our best interests to act accordingly. Cats, after all, can offer an easy path to the doghouse.

- She wants to have a cat, so you tolerate the cat. **0**
- But in order to have the cat, you must give up your dog. **+15**
- You've had Scruffy since you were in your teens. **+17**
- He knew many tricks. **+20**
- He knew how to play dead. **+21**
- He's not playing anymore. **+30**

- You are nice to her cat even though it does not acknowledge your existence. **+2**
- It leaves Friskies all over the kitchen **+7**
- and those little pellets get stuck between your toes. **+8**
- But you admit they taste pretty good with ketchup. **–22**

- Still, when asked, you feed her cat. **+5**
- When your mate is looking, you pet the cat. **+5**
- You actually let the cat sleep on your belly while you watch ESPN. **+8**
- Your mate can't believe how calm the cat has been around you lately. **+15**
- She's also wondering what happened to the cough syrup. **–15**

- You carry the cat like a baby. **+2**
- You carry the cat like a doctor's bag. **–8**

- When your mate tells cat stories at various parties, you stand quietly and nod with a smile of resignation on your face. **+5**
- When she tells cat stories, you actually chime in with a few of them yourself. **+6**
- When your mate tells these unending cat stories, you chime in about how tender the meat is when they're still kittens. **−8**

- You suggest testing the "cats always land on their feet" theory **−60**
- from a moving car. **−135**

....

AIRPORT ETIQUETTE

When it comes to picking up your mate at the airport, she gets off the plane with more than her Louis Vuitton. She touches down loaded with expectations. Are you smart enough to meet them?

- When she returns home on a flight, you meet her right at the gate. **+4**
- When she gets in, you meet her right at the gate, holding flowers. **+5**
- When she gets in, you tell her you'll meet her at baggage claim, but you actually surprise her by meeting her at the gate **+6**
- with flowers and mineral water, too **+8**
- and some premoistened towelettes. **+9**
- And Uma, the masseuse, you met on Concourse C. **−131**

- When the two of you were first dating, you used to pick her up at the gate all the time, but now you meet her at baggage claim. **0**
- Now you meet her out front. **−20**
- And she carries her bags to the car. **−40**
- At least you honk to let her know where you are. **−55**

VEGETARIANISM

Studies show that when women become vegetarians, they not only lose weight, they also lose their sense of humor. Perhaps humor is only found in animal proteins.

- Your mate is a vegetarian because she doesn't like to harm animals, and you "really respect that." **+3**
- You never point out that while she's telling you this she's twiddling the buttons on her leather coat. **+5**

- When you dine with her, you always order vegetarian as a sign of support. **+9**
- When you dine with her, you still eat meat **−8**
- and you *enjoy* it. **−10**
- You even eat veal in front of her **−20**
- but not before giving it an affectionate name. **−45**
- Fluffy. **−60**

- Your mate is a vegetarian, so you decide to give up beef also, just to make her happy. **+15**
- You even take classes in vegetarian cooking. **+16**

- You now know a special dish that uses tofu and exotic ingredients. **+22**
- The cat's missing. **−100**

YOUR SPECIAL TALENTS

We all possess certain traits that make us different from everyone else. And those of us who are not blessed with such traits go on to successful careers in politics.

- You can cook at least one meal really well. **+5**
- You can actually cook a number of different things really, really well. **+10**
- You're a better cook than her. **−10**

- You can mix a perfect martini. **+1**
- You can mix the perfect Harvey Wallbanger. **−5**
- You can mix a decent can of paint. **−8**

- You're not a bad tennis player. **+15**
- You're not a bad golfer. **−15**
- You're really good at board games. **−10**
- Yahtzee is your specialty. **−50**

- You can speak two languages. **+5**
- One of them is Klingon. **−20**

- You have an advanced degree **+10**
- from the automotive college that advertises on cable at 3 A.M. **−10**

- You are good with your hands, **+15**
- which means you don't own a computer. **–10**

- You grow your own vegetables in the backyard. **+10**
- You grow your own vegetables in your sock drawer. **–10**

- You have a wonderful voice, and you delight in entertaining guests with renditions of Broadway show tunes. **+10**
- You have a horrible voice, and you prove it daily by singing to the radio. **–25**
- Even when it's off. **–50**

- You are an accomplished hunter. **–15**
- You are an accomplished painter. **+15**
- Your works are hanging at a gallery. **+30**
- Your kills are hanging above the fireplace. **–30**

- You write poetry. **+10**
- You write dirty limericks **–10**
- and recite them at the church picnic. **–55**

- You take up a religion. **0**
- It's a cool, Middle-Eastern religion. **+25**
- You burn incense and contemplate great spiritual topics. **+40**
- You shave your head and hang out at the airport. **–150**

- You collect expensive things like automobiles, watches, or works of art. **+100**
- You collect really boring things like rare coins, stamps, or butterflies. **–50**

- You collect NFL pro-football drinking glasses from the local gas station. **−100**
- Where you work. **−200**

- You practice yoga. **+20**
- You say it brings you closer to inner peace. **+25**
- Actually, you just like watching the women in class bend over. **−24**

- You can play at least one song on the guitar. **+5**
- You can play at least one song on the piano. **+10**
- You can play at least one song on the violin. **+20**
- You can play at least one song on your comb. **−20**
- You swear it's an icebreaker at parties. **−30**

....

CHAPTER SUMMARY:
WHAT HAVE WE LEARNED?

1. Her birthday is an important event for both of you. Do not ruin it by purchasing yet another pair of edible undies. Get something she can wear this time.
2. Ex-girlfriends are like dinner napkins. When you know you're finished, get them off your lap.
3. The only good ex-boyfriend is a broke, drugged out, balding ex-boyfriend. The worst ex-boyfriend, however, is a dead one. You can't compete with a dead ex-boyfriend.
4. Even though you hate her cat, it's her cat, so be nice to the cat. Stop feeding it Brillo pads.

5. If your woman is a vegetarian, then respect her decision. Stop fondling the pot roasts at the supermarket.
6. Cultivate a special talent. Make it something that does not involve cupping your hand around your armpit.

....

YOUR SCORECARD GIFT SHOP

What you get for what you did.

- Buy her an expensive dinner + see a movie of her choice = one vigorous sex act.
- Buy her an expensive dinner + see a movie of her choice + a gift of expensive jewelry = two traditional sex acts + one experimental sex act.
- Buy her an expensive dinner + see a movie of her choice + one gift of expensive jewelry – one crack about her hair = cold shoulder that night.

2 THE ART OF LIVING TOGETHER

You've known her for a while. Most of your clothes are at her place. Most of her clothes are at your place. Her refrigerator is empty because you've eaten everything in sight (including her roommate's heart medication), and your refrigerator is jammed with moldy life forms that would shame most rainforests. By now, both of you figure this dating thing is getting a bit redundant.

So she's thinking, hey, why spend all our money on two rent bills? Why don't we move in together?

- You move in with her. **+175**
- She moves in with you. **−200**

Remember, she likes to keep her things right where they are. Moreover, if things don't work out, it's you who has to vacate. That says a lot about the risk you're taking. As well as the allure of sleeping on clean sheets for a change.

....

FAST POINTERS FOR LIVING WITH A MEMBER
OF THE OPPOSITE SEX (I.E., WOMEN)

Below are the fifteen major mistakes that can occur when you are living together. These simple pointers are based on decades of scientific research rigorously performed at many prisons across the country.

1. *You destroy the Daily Herald. –3*

Try to refrain from mutilating, tearing up, staining, or crumpling the newspaper before she reads it. No one likes to read the paper after it's been smeared with grape jam, or worse, your own blood. And don't leave sections on the bathroom floor.

2. *You aren't Mr. Sunshine. –3*

If you rarely say good morning in the morning, you are overlooking a very easy opportunity to start off the day on a good foot. Or on any foot. Greeting her in the morning is polite, civilized, and it reminds her you're aware she's still around. Which is a good thing, if she's horny.

3. *You surprise her often. –3*

Women hate to be startled. When that happens, they immediately gain three pounds.

4. *You disrupt her. –3*

If she has a favorite TV show, don't interrupt her when she's watching it. Instead, pretend to like it, even if it is dreadful.

Anything on the Lifetime Channel qualifies, as well as made-for-TV dramas that portray men as evil, loathsome creatures. She likes these shows because they make her feel better about her situation. Cherish that.

5. You tell friends about her fascination with the men on the Weather Channel. –25

Never reveal any of her unusual habits or quirks to pals or other members of the family. Remember, you have more to hide than she does. We've seen your files.

6. You don't call her by her first name. –4

She has one, you know. And never, ever call her "Mom." You don't have sex with your mother, do you? Don't answer that.

7. You don't offer her half of your BLT. –5

Whenever you're making food for yourself, always offer to make some for her. She may not want any, but offer her some anyway. Moreover, you may get lucky: offer to make her something, and there's a chance she'll actually come in the kitchen and do the work for you.

8. You start arguments in front of Aunt Helga. –7

Never initiate an argument in front of her friends, your friends, her family, your family, members of the clergy, or elite paramilitary outfits. Of course, she can start an argument with you, but love is not a two-way street. It is more like a blind alley, filled with snakes and candy samplers.

9. You like to try on her clothes. −42

Stop that.

10. You rarely answer the door. −6

It is your responsibility to handle all inquisitors who come to the door. Meaning: salesmen, leafleteers, members of Greenpeace, sinister paperboys, born-agains, unbalanced neighbors, well-armed terrorists. Memorize these three words: "Nope, not interested." Take special pride in slamming the door. If there happens to be a group at the door, feel free to scatter them with pepper spray. It's a "laff riot!" −7

11. You have houseguests. −8

Never have houseguests.

12. You make the bed the easy way. −6

Making the bed requires more than throwing the bedspread over the blankets. Do it right, and make sure she's out of the bed first.

13. You do not understand the one single rule that applies to farting. −8

And you've probably already violated it. Many times.

14. You engage in nasty habits. −8

Here's the rule: leave her presence (perhaps sneak to another room), and scratch to your heart's content. Then return.

15. You're mean to her friends. –9

Only be mean to the ones whom you know are saying bad things about you (that narrows it down to all of them).

....

FRIENDS

Chances are many of your friends have all but fallen off the radar screen. This is typical. As you become more and more involved in a relationship, you end up seeing less and less of them. And of course, some of them are simply not out on parole yet.

This is not how it works when it comes to her friends. Not only does she hold onto them during a relationship, they seem to multiply like so many third-rate movies starring a Baldwin brother. These strange creatures rear their ugly heads frequently—usually for hours at a time—drinking diet drinks, moaning about Antonio Banderas's gluteus maximus and talking about their fibromyalgia (whatever that is). *Worse, they talk about you.*

The point is simple.

If you still have friends, they will cost you points. If she still has friends, they will cost you points, too.

It's up to you, however, to minimize the damage.

- You have one or two close friends, but thankfully, they are married and fairly docile. **0**
- You still have one single friend left, and it's pretty obvious why he is still unmarried. **–10**
- But you don't talk to him anymore **+5**
- not until the trial ends, anyway. **–5**

- You have a few friends, but only because they are married or dating friends of your mate. **+5**
- Without them, though, you'd have absolutely no social life at all. **+9**
- Well, except for the hand puppets. **−20**

- You set up one of your single friends with one of your mate's single friends. **+3**
- Her friend is never seen or heard from again. **−45**

- Actually, the set-up is quite a success. **+2**
- They move in together. **+10**
- Your friend seems to treat her better than you treat your mate. **−10**
- And her friend never lets her forget it. **−15**

- Your friends tend to visit you often. **−7**
- At odd hours. **−15**
- At least they always bring something to the house. **+3**
- Usually, a ripe odor. **−16**

- One of your friends likes to come over and hang out on the front lawn and drink beer. **−22**
- You'd tell him to leave, but you do the same thing at his house. **−34**

- When with your friends, you aren't afraid to act romantic toward your mate. **+5**
- You hug and kiss her in front of them. **+6**
- You make go-goo eyes. **+15**
- You talk in baby talk. **+20**

- And you wonder why they like to perform wheelies on your front lawn at 3 A.M. **–25**

THE PRECARIOUS USE OF BABY TALK

Give a relationship time to evolve, and a completely normal woman will soon reject traditional modes of communication and instead begin to "baby talk." Mind you, there are no babies in a three-mile radius. But this doesn't stop these otherwise perfectly adjusted females from suddenly talking like Smurfs on cough syrup. It is very annoying—yet it continues, unabated, like those cooking shows on public television.

But the question is, when your partner does it, are you required to join in?

It depends. You will certainly lose the respect of your friends if they catch you doing it. But you must realize women baby talk for a reason, either to test our willingness to succumb to their every whim, or to see how far we'll go to get laid. But if that's one way to get sex, then we're all for it.

- You use baby talk with your partner only when you're alone. **+1**
- You baby talk in front of strangers **+2**
- in front of coworkers **+17**
- in front of her friends **+21**
- in front of your friends **+50**
- in front of your single friends **+75**

- when it's clear you're dying inside **+85**
- You come up with baby talk nicknames for each other **+15**
- "Snookums" or "Poopie." **+20**
- You use them privately. **+4**
- You use them publicly. **+6**
- They're on your greeting cards. **+15**

- You employ baby talk when snuggling in bed. **+5**
- You employ baby talk when discussing her minor injury: "Ooooh . . . did you get a boo-boo?" **+3**
- You employ baby talk when discussing her major injury: "Oooh . . . did little snookums fracture her third vertebra?" **−24**

- When your friends are over, you always put her needs ahead of theirs. **+10**
- You turn down requests to play golf, because the two of you planned to shop for new candle holders. **+15.**
- You turn down requests to play poker, because it's "whoopie" night. **0**
- But it's clear on your face that you'd rather play poker. **−15**

- Her friends visit often, and they tend to stay for hours at a time. **0**
- When they visit, you stay and keep them company. **+4**
- You don't keep them company; instead you immediately duck out to the garage. **−4**
- But you don't have a garage. **−6**
- You begin building one. **−12**

- When her friends visit, you make polite conversation. **+5**
- You fetch them snack foods and assorted diet drinks. **+7**
- You listen to them talk about their current relationship disasters. **+10**
- You don't make fun of their weight problems. **+5**
- Although you make a point to have them sit on the stable chairs. **−8**

- Your mate has one friend that you don't mind. **+1**
- You always tell her she should get into modeling. **−14**
- You then saunter around casually with a Minolta. **−33**

THE GOOD, THE BAD, AND THE PIANO

There are some movies she loves, and some you hate. And then there are movies you adore, which are usually located in a special room, behind a curtain in your local video store. But here is the real dilemma: while she is not at all required to sit through any of your movie picks, you are expected to sit through hers. All in the name of points. Just so you know: a woman flick must satisfy all of the following requirements.

- It must feature a defiant heroine (Cher, Bette Midler, Whoopi Goldberg or Sally Field) who overcomes all odds (meaning an abusive, moronic boyfriend) to find a new sense of identity (meaning turn into a raging lesbian).

- It must star Daniel Day Lewis, Patrick Swayze, or Hugh Grant as a sensitive soul who makes the rest of us look really bad by comparison. He does this by making the heroine something out of clay.
- It must have a sappy soundtrack, with painful ballads by monstrosities like Mariah Carey or Michael Bolton.
- There must be at least three fits of crying (two of them by men).
- It should be based on a book you were required to read in college or high school, but didn't because you were always drunk.
- It should be based on a true story with real social implications. The climax might involve a march past the White House.

Here are the real point gainers. Rent them and be prepared to talk about them after viewing.

- *The Piano.* Gleefully pushes all the feminist buttons. You get extra points for Harvey Keitel's ghoulish frontal nudity. **+3**
- *Sleepless in Seattle.* Every woman likes to think she's Meg Ryan (even if she looks like Bette Midler). **+3**
- *When Harry Met Sally.* More of Meg, plus it capitalizes on the female notion that if all else fails, you can always hook up with your best pal. **+3**
- *Steel Magnolias.* One of the many films that functions as a two-hour slumber party: get a bunch of women together and let the giggle fits begin. Bring Pepto for the sad ending. **+3**

- *Sense and Sensibility.* More costume changes than the Ziegfield Follies. She'll like that. **+5**
- *Singles.* Great soundtrack. Chicks love movies with great soundtracks. And Matt Dillon? Dreamy! **+5**
- *Little Women.* Has women in it. Plus it's a book every woman probably read. Caution: she'll reread the book, and then want to tell you about it. Over latte. **+5**
- *Thelma and Louise.* Ideal for angry women who listen to Alanis Morissette. If your mate really, really likes this movie, begin sleeping with the light on. **+6**
- *The Unbearable Lightness of Being.* Unbearably long and tedious. But points are scored for a Daniel Day Lewis appearance. **+6**
- *Ghost.* Demi makes pottery with a dead guy: every woman's dream. **+7**
- *How To Make an American Quilt.* Has "quilt" in the title. That just about covers it. **+7**
- *Four Weddings and a Funeral.* This made Hugh Grant's career. Enough said. **+7**
- *First Wives Club.* Revenge fantasy combined with women-in-a-group-stuff. Points for ghastly Bette Midler sighting. **+7**
- *Three Men and a Baby.* A baby flick always scores points with women, unless it's *Rosemary's Baby.* **+7**
- *Benny and Joon.* Johnny Depp is so deep! **+7**
- *Mermaids.* Packed to the gills with rickety Cher and winsome Winona Ryder. That kind of chick flick synergy is bound to score points! **+7**

GUY FLICKS THAT WILL COST YOU POINTS

A guy movie must satisfy only one requirement: It must star Arnold, Mel, Clint, or Bruce as a rebel figure who bucks the system and does things his own way, while killing dozens of creeps and delivering clever catch phrases in the process. It may include gratuitous but very brief scenes of nudity—as long as it doesn't detract from the mayhem. Here are the ones that will cost you dearly.

- *Fistful of Dollars.* Clint, guns, and tightly wrapped cigars. Not big favorites among the bra and panty set. **–2**
- *Walking Tall.* Women love romance, we love revenge. With a baseball bat. **–2**
- *Caddyshack.* Most women hate golf, so expect them to hate movies about golf. **–3**
- *Deliverance.* Ned Beatty's best "roll." **–4**
- *Dirty Harry.* Justice, Clint-style. His vigilante sensibilities may offend the tenderhearted. **–4**
- *True Romance.* You may be able to fool her with the title, but there's gore galore! **–5**
- *Reanimator.* Cunnilingus performed by a headless guy! Talk about mixing the good with the bad. She'll hate this. **–5**
- *Road Warrior.* Finger-slicing scene will cost you digits, too! **–5**
- *Alien.* Lots of oozing gore. Sure, the hero is a woman, but anything that oozes costs you points. **–5**
- *Silence of the Lambs.* Serve steak kabobs afterward, and you're grounded for life. **–5**

- *The Terminator.* She probably enjoyed this once, but not by the seventh viewing. **-5**
- *Hellraiser.* Show her the cover with the pinhead monster, and tell her it's about sewing. **-6**
- *Guns, Girls, and Gangsters.* Never saw it, but figure the title alone will cost you points. **-7**
- *How to Murder Your Wife.* See above. **-15**
- *The Texas Chainsaw Massacre.* Studies show women are not fond of movies about cannibalism. **-20**
- *Scanners.* When a head explodes—your stock plummets. **-22**
- *DeathRace 2000.* The plot: a crosscountry race in which drivers accrue points by running over invalids. If your mate doesn't find this repulsive, keep her away from your grandparents. **-23**
- *A Boy and His Dog.* Starring Don Johnson, it may be the most reviled guy movie ever. Why? If I told you, I would spoil the ending! **-25**

YOUR CLOSET

Clothing certainly makes the man, but only if the woman approves. As a rule, wear everything she buys for you—even if it makes you look silly, or worse, like Regis Philbin.

- You own a navy blazer. **+6**
- It still looks new **+3**
- because you never wear it. **-6**

- You own a navy blazer. **+6**
- It still has barf stains on the lapel from the frat days. **–5**
- You call them "the good old days." **–9**

- You own one designer suit. **+8**
- You only wear it on job interviews. **–4**
- That means you wear it regularly. **–6**
- To fast-food restaurants. **–29**

- You own a sports coat. **+5**
- You own a house coat. **–15**
- And no house. **–75**

- You own a week's worth of tailored dress shirts. **+6**
- You own a week's worth of short-sleeved dress shirts **–12**
- with a matching clip-on tie for each one. **–22**
- Three of them are novelty ties. **–35**
- One of them plays music. **–45**
- "Dancing Queen." **–175**

- You own two pairs of formal shoes. **+16**
- You own a nice pair of loafers. **+7**
- You only own shoes with the latest in airpump technology. **–9**
- And you don't play basketball. **–12**

- You own a nice watch **+10**
- You own a digital watch with lots of cool buttons. **–13**
- It can play the theme to *Close Encounters of the Third Kind*. **–23**

- You own satin boxers. **+6**
- You own white briefs. **–15**
- You believe turning them inside out is just the same as cleaning them. **–60**

- You own a few comfortable, oversized sweaters she loves to wear **+15**
- until she finds long blonde hairs on them. **−10**
- And short ones, too. **−45**

- You own at least one piece of clothing with a professional sports logo or mascot on it. **−2**
- All you own is clothing with professional sports logos or mascots. **−50**
- Because you're a professional athlete. **+100**
- Because you sell hot dogs at the stadium. **−45**

- You own one baseball cap with great sentimental value. **+2**
- You own a lot of baseball caps. **−8**
- And you never take them off. **−20**
- Except when trading them at swap meets. **−40**

- You own sweatpants **−5**
- and you never do anything that would cause you to sweat. **−10**

- You own shirts with the names of rock bands on them, **−10**
- speed metal rock bands. **−20**
- They're black long-sleeved shirts with world tour dates emblazoned on the back. **−25**
- And you're not a concert promotor. **−40**
- You're an accountant. **−45**

··

TELEVISION

When it comes to the idiot box, you are required to watch what she likes. It doesn't matter how maudlin or sappy or ridiculous, it is part and parcel of the relationship. She is, however, not expected to reciprocate. Rule of thumb: watching a "very special" episode of "Blossom" or anything else will always earn you points.

- In your spare time, you take great comfort in watching:
- whatever she is watching **+10**
- figure skating **+15**
- educational or culturally sophisticated television **+3**
- we mean the boring stuff on PBS **+3**

- bass fishing or angling shows **–3**
- the Golf Channel **–3**
- stock-car racing **–4**
- talk shows devoted to stock-car racing **–6**

- The Playboy Channel **–15**
- The Playboy Channel, scrambled **–20**

- ESPN **–22**
- ESPN, scrambled **–25**

- professional football **–25**
- professional bowling **–30**
- professional arm wrestling **–45**
- Fran Tarkenton infomercials **–145**

- "Cops" **–33**
- "Cops" reruns **–35**
- "Cops," but only when you're on it **–40**

SHE OFTEN FINDS YOU READING . . .

- quietly in the den as a means of relaxation **+5**
- only when you're on the toilet **–34**

When you're in the bathroom, you read . . .

- *The Economist* **+7**
- the *Wall Street Journal* **+4**
- the sports pages **–5**
- *Soldier of Fortune* **–17**
- *TV Guide* **–3**
- *The Classic Compendium of Hustler Humor* **–45**
- her diary **–176**

THE USE AND ABUSE OF THE TELEPHONE

Men don't hate the telephone. It's just that it seems no woman's ear is complete without one.

- The phone rings during dinner and you answer it. **0**
- You talk on the phone for over ten minutes. **–10**
- When your mate asks you who it was, you tell her it was a wrong number. **–25**

- You tell her she has a phone call. **0**
- She can't come to the phone, she says, because she's on the toilet. **–2**

- You tell the caller she can't come to the phone because she's on the toilet. **–15**

- You tell her she has a phone call and she wants to know who it is.
- You tell her, and she emphatically states, "Tell her I'm not home." **0**
- You tell the caller, "She says she's not home." **–19**
- You end up talking about her for 45 minutes. **–50**

THE TYPE OF PHONE

Sometimes, it's what you dial that makes her smile.

- You own a cell phone. **+3**
- You own a cordless phone. **+2**
- You own a rotary phone. **–2**
- You own a phone that looks like a model of a Corvette. **–5**
- You own a phone that rests inside a football helmet. **–10**
- You got it for subscribing to *Sports Illustrated.* **–15**

CHAPTER SUMMARY:
WHAT HAVE WE LEARNED?

- The moment you move in with a woman is the same moment you can kiss your boxful of *Penthouse Forum*s goodbye. As well as your "furniture."

- Keep a safe distance from her friends at all times. Especially the cute ones. They're more trouble than you think. Don't tell them you're a modeling agent.
- Get used to the idea of never seeing any of your close friends again. Consider imaginary playmates instead. Sew two buttons on a sock, and you're there!
- The bathroom is not a place for conversation, especially if you're the only one in there.
- Watching sports on television is fine as long as it's Torvill and Dean skating "Bolero." For the seventy-fifth time.

THE SCORECARD GIFT SHOP

Here's what you get for what you did.

- You put on nice clothes to go shopping for groceries = you get to pick the flavor of Pop Tarts.
- You tell a dirty joke in public = one viewing of a very special episode of "Dr. Quinn, Medicine Woman."
- You are nice to her friends = She tolerates your friends.
- You flirt with her friends = Clean the gutters + eat canned soup for dinner.
- You throw out all your sweaty baseball caps = one Chuck Norris film.
- You rent one movie starring Barbra Streisand = you rent any movie not starring Barbra Streisand.

3

MOUTH TO MOUTH: THE ART OF COMMUNICATION

Perhaps your mate comes to you with that serious look on her face. The one that screams those four famous words "We need to talk." Fine. You don't agree, and you feel awkward, but you're more than willing to sit down and listen intently as she expresses her feelings. Things seem to be going well as you listen to her express her misgivings about you, her job, her parents, her brief fling with the surviving members of Menudo.

When she is done expressing her feelings, you feel compelled—almost emboldened—to make an effort to talk to her about a problem you've been having.

But after you bare your soul, you are met with a blank stare.

Congratulations. You have learned a valuable lesson. Your problems are not her problems. So keep them to yourself, or call a psychic hotline. Dionne Warwick is waiting.

....

SERIOUS TALK

- When she wants to talk about a problem, you listen intently. **0**
- You hold her hand throughout. **+4**
- You try to change the subject by unbuttoning her blouse. **−14**
- In Kmart. **−47**

- When she wants to talk about a problem you listen intently, and you display what looks like a concerned expression. **+5**
- You are able to maintain that concerned expression for over thirty minutes. **+4**
- You even nod intently at times. **+5**
- You are able to listen to her for at least an hour. **+8**
- You never pick up a newspaper, paperback, or girlie magazine. **+5**
- You never glance at the television, out the window, or turn on the CD player. **+7**
- She realizes this is because you have fallen asleep. **−25**

- When she wants to talk about a problem, you listen intently. **0**
- You listen intently, and you even offer insightful comments concerning her predicament. **+3**
- In fact, your insightful comments make *too much* sense. **−6**
- She tells you to butt out. **−12**

- She says something meaningful to you, expecting a response. **0**
- You say, "I understand." **+2**
- Actually, you say nothing. **−10**

- This is because you refuse to remove the Walkman. **–15**
- This is because she's a good shot with the vase. **–20**

- You talk to your mate a lot. **+6**
- You talk to yourself a lot more. **–45**

- You share your dreams with your mate. **+5**
- No, not your dreams of the future, but the dumb dreams you had last night. **–6**
- The ones that always take place in high school and you're walking around naked with a goat **–25**
- and you forgot about the midterm exam. **–30**

- She asks you a question. **0**
- You say nothing. **–6**
- She asks you the same question again. **–8**
- You say, "I heard you the first time." **–15**

....

PERMISSIBLE SMALL TALK

While you can say just about anything you want to a buddy (short of "I dreamt about you last night, naked and eating a banana"), with women it's a whole different bag of snakes. Honesty is irrelevant, the right answer almost always proves wrong, and the golden rule is this: Don't dig a hole deeper than the one you are already in.

So, here's the score for:

- airing dirty laundry about other people **+5**
- airing dirty laundry about you and her **–20**
- airing dirty laundry you didn't know was dirty in the first place **–25**

- like the time you and her got drunk and took off your clothes and . . . **−74**
- actually showing friends your dirty laundry **−150**

Announcing casually to anyone in particular that
- "I am so lucky to have this woman as my girlfriend." **+6**
- "I am so lucky my girlfriend ignores my transgressions." **−2**
- "My girlfriend has diarrhea." **−30**

- Saying "Are you going to eat that?" **−3**
- to your mate **−2**
- to her employer **−8**
- to a complete stranger **−9**
- to a homeless guy **−20**

Starting off any joke with:
- "So this guy walks into a bar . . ." **−10**
- "So this (*insert ethnic group here*) guy walks into a bar . . ." **−100**
- "So this (*insert ethnic group here*) guy, and a (*insert ethnic group here*) guy and a (*insert ethnic group here*) guy are on a desert island . . ." **−170**

- Anything about sports. **−5**
- "How 'bout those #$*%# Redskins!" **−20**
- "How 'bout those #$*%# (anything)!" **−20**
- Anything during sex. **−75**

- anything about a TV show you watched last night that she didn't see **−6**
- recounting the entire plot line of a movie you and your mate just saw that she didn't like **−8**
- recounting any long embarrassing stories that end in "and she just about died!" **−30**

- relating any story that happened at work that was supposed to be funny **–6**
- ending the story with, "You really gotta meet these guys— they're a riot!" **–12**

- calling her "mom" **–35**
- calling her "mommy" **–40**
- calling her "babe" **–45**
- calling her "jugs" **–50**
- calling her at 4 A.M., drunk **–75**

- referring in any way to her weight **–40**
- referring in any way to your sex life **–45**
- referring in any way to her family **–50**
- referring in any way to her family's sex life **–55**
- on "Oprah" **–250**
- Saying anything about her cooking, even if you mean it as a compliment **–25** (Example: You: "My wife makes a terrific lasagna." Her: "What's the matter, you don't like my meat-loaf?")

WHAT'S YOUR LINE? A CONVERSATIONAL PRIMER

Think you can think fast on your feet? Then prove it.

When a famous female political leader is on the television, you say:

A. "You know, she's really amazing. Too bad there aren't more like her." **+2**
B. "I'd do her." **–5**
C. "She's fat . . . but I'd do her." **–10**

When you meet one of your partner's best friends for the first time, you say:

A. "Nice to finally meet you. Suzette has told me so many great things about you." +2

B. "Funny, you don't look depressed." –18

When she complains to a waiter, and the waiter looks to you, you say:

A. "You heard her, this meal is unacceptable. Please do something about it promptly." +3

B. "Hey, see what I gotta deal with everyday?" –20

When she asks you if you want to have kids, you say:

A. "I'm not sure if I'm ready, but when I am, I'd want them with you." +2

B. "Do I want kids? Yeah, sometimes. But sadly, our society frowns upon such relationships." –31

She asks you to give her "your honest opinion."

A. You lie through your teeth. 0

B. You actually give her your honest opinion. –15

C. You fake an aneurism. –20

She asks you how many lovers you've had before.

A. You say, "Before when?" –10

B. You keep the number under five. –13

C. You start counting fingers. **−27**

D. You move to your toes. **−45**

E. You're on your fifth lap. **−110**

F. You pause and ask, "Men, women, or both?" **−178**

G. "Does the year in Thailand count?" **−300**

She asks you if you like her hair the way it is, and you reply:

A. "Honey, it looks great." **+2**

B. "Don't worry, it will grow out." **−7**

C. "I liked it better when it was all one color." **−14**

D. "Didn't David Bowie wear that shade for the Ziggy Stardust tour?" **−47**

She asks you about your religious preference, and you reply:

A. "Faith has always been a personal thing to me." **0**

B. "Mmmm . . . I like the one where the guy turns water into wine." **−10**

THE MOST DANGEROUS QUESTION YOU'LL EVER HAVE TO FACE

- She asks, "Do I look fat?" **−5** (a question like this one is so sensitive, you immediately start with a deficit)
- You hesitate in responding. **−10**

- You reply, "Where?" **−25**
- You reply, "What? Are you pregnant?" **−30**

THE SECOND MOST DANGEROUS QUESTION YOU'LL EVER HAVE TO FACE

She asks, "Does this (dress, shirt, skirt, house coat, car tarp) make me look fat?"

- You hesitate in responding. **−10**
- You say, "Not from the side view, hon." **−15**
- You say, "Only with the lights on." **−20**
- You say, "No hon, your body just makes the dress look wide." **−40**

SENSE OF HUMOR

If you want to communicate effectively with your mate, it helps to make her laugh. A little levity here and there can help ease her burdens and take her mind off her thighs. But there are limits. Make too many jokes, and soon she will say "Everything is just a big joke, isn't it?"

Again, she's right. Everything *is* a big joke to us.

Below are some common mistakes men make when they try to appear funny in front of their mate. Commit these gaffes, and you're destined for a stay in the doghouse.

1. You don't know how to edit. –6

Whatever may be funny to you or your buddies as you sit around drinking warm Pabst will most certainly make her cringe. Example: jokes about kids eaten by snakes. We all love those. Women hate them.

2. You tell really long, meandering jokes. –8

A joke that never ends alienates everyone around you, especially women. That's because they take up valuable time that could be better filled with pointless gossip, obsessive shopping excursions, and meaningless long distance phone conversations with friends they don't really like.

3. You bring home the dirty jokes you heard from your coworkers. –9

How do you know when a joke should not be told to a woman? Any joke that ends with "It tastes funny."

4. You believe everyone really enjoys it when you do your Bill Murray imitation from Caddyshack. –10

They don't.

5. You falsely believe that what she finds funny privately she also finds humorous in public. –30

Almost everything you say to make her giggle when you're lying in bed will get you in deep trouble if you say it to her in front of her friends, parents, grandparents, or household pets.

She has an image to preserve. And you don't help by talking about the nicknames both of you have for your genitals. Even if they're cute.

6. You use props. –35

Notice how you never hear from Gallagher anymore?

....

RISKY, DIRTY, AND DUMB HUMOR

Stuff you say, shouldn't say, or wish you could say.

- You never make jokes about individuals less fortunate than you. **+10**
- Because they're aren't any individuals less fortunate than you. **–10**

- You never tell dirty jokes. **+15**
- Except around the table at Christmas dinner. **–15**

- You tell jokes that begin, "What do you call a guy with no arms and no legs" **–2**
- You tell these jokes while visiting a VA hospital. **–300**

- You tell a mildly dirty joke to her in private **–2**
- and she giggles. **+3**
- You tell the very same joke to her, in front of others **–5**
- and she doesn't giggle. **–13**
- And you follow up quickly with, "See, isn't that just awful?" **–15**

- You tell any joke that lasts longer than four minutes. **–10**
- You screw up the punchline. **–50**

- You own T-shirts with so-called humorous sayings. **–10**
- "I'm with Stupid." **–15**
- "I am Stupid." **–16**

- You own at least one coffee mug with a humorous saying about work on it. **–2**
- "A bad day of fishing beats a good day at work." **–3**
- And you don't have a job. **–10**

- You own at least one baseball cap with a humorous saying on it. **–15**
- "Official Bikini Inspector." **–20**
- You actually are a bikini inspector. **–30**

- You do impressions. **–5**
- You do them at parties, where you think everyone enjoys them. **–40**
- You're especially proud of your Katharine Hepburn. **–25**
- It gives you a chance to dress up. **–50**

WHAT WOMEN FIND FUNNY

- the "For Better Or Worse" comic strip
- "Ziggy"
- "Cathy"
- Probably one of those guys on "Friends"
- animals playfully wrestling on nature shows

- adorable anecdotes about their cats' antics
- Rosie O'Donnell, on a Krispy Kreme binge
- Tom Hanks
- the stupid things their friends say

WHAT WOMEN DON'T FIND FUNNY

- the Three Stooges
- breaking wind
- 95 percent of what comes out of Howard Stern's mouth
- jokes based on airline disasters, celebrity tragedies, or the freakish maiming of any member of the animal kingdom
- slapstick
- joy buzzers and those cans you open and snakes pop out
- jokes about her career or lack thereof
- fat jokes, even if they aren't directed at her
- jokes regarding the fact that it "must be her time of the month"

UNFUNNY THINGS BOTH MEN AND WOMEN AGREE ON

- Weird Al Yankovich
- John Ritter
- commercials featuring Candace Bergen
- Carrot Top
- Pauly Shore
- reruns of "Night Court"
- the last ten years of "Saturday Night Live"

- morning zoo deejays
- improvisational comedy
- dopes who think it's funny to yell out "Freebird!" at any musical event

YOUR VIEWS ON STERN

When the topic of Howard Stern comes up, you're always quick to say,

- "I find him quite vulgar." **+8**
- "He's just another example of how low our country's tastes have sunk." **+9**
- "I can't stand the way he continually degrades women. He's obviously sexist garbage." **+15**
- "Does that guy have the life or what!" **−10**

ARGUMENTS

Watch any daytime talk show, and invariably you will find some freakish-looking Ph.D. type with a hyphenated name imploring us more ignorant folk to "fight fair." It certainly sounds democratic, but unfortunately it does not work.

Here's why: fighting fair means completely different things to men and women. To men, fighting fair involves both you and your mate expressing your feelings, trying to work out your disagreements, making up, and then making out.

To your mate, however, fighting fair boils down to this: she tells you why you are wrong and you agree 100 percent.

Then she tells you again.

- When arguing you are always quick to see her point of view **+5**
- as you leave to go bowling. **−9**

- When arguing, you never admit you are wrong. **−15**
- When arguing, you always admit you are wrong. **+7**
- Even when you weren't in the car when she plowed into the lemonade stand. **+20**

- When arguing, you slip in cheap shots **−20**
- about her weight **−30**
- about her parents **−40**
- about her extensive collection of Yanni CDs. **−45**

- You bring up something she did in the past that was unsavory, just to get her mad **−15**
- like the time she was caught shoplifting **−35**
- like her four-year stay at the institution **−55**
- like the time she first slept with you. **−75**

- When arguing, she slips in cheap shots about you. **+5**
- You let them slide. **+15**
- You take them as a compliment. **−15**

When she says "We don't communicate anymore,"
- You say, "You're so right. I'm very, very sorry." **+1**
- You say, "No thanks, I'll grab something at work." **−5**

TIFFS THAT WILL COST YOU POINTS

It doesn't matter who's wrong or right: these quarrels will cost you bigtime—in points and in sex.

- You argue about money. **−20**
- You argue about her parents. **−30**
- You argue about your lack of ambition or job prospects. **−40**
- You argue about her ability—or lack thereof—to parallel park. **−60**
- You argue over the artistic merit of Kenny G. **−80**

BEST RESPONSES TO HER ANGRY QUESTIONS

- "You're right, dear." **+1**
- "You're absolutely right dear." **+2**
- "My goodness, how foolish of me. Well, you're right again, dear!" **+3**
- "Oh, yes. Yes. Yes. Yes." **+4**

YOUR OPINIONS ON HER PERSONAL TASTE

- You agree that M. Scott Peck is a tremendous writer. **+2**
- You laugh out loud when you read the sections she's highlighted in his book. **−15**

- You tell her that, yes, Alanis Morissette's music is very powerful and moving. **+3**
- You can't explain why only her CDs disappear when there's a "break-in." **−15**

- You agree with her that "Melrose Place" does have social merit in underscoring the emotional troubles that face many young men and women today. **+4**
- You only watch it just in case Heather Locklear puts on anything skimpy. **–5**

HOW YOU SCORE WHEN YOU EXPRESS NO OPINION ON:

- the feminist movement **–10**
- the environment **–12**
- social problems **–15**
- world hunger **–20**
- her new outfit **–30**
- her new hairstyle **–50**

HOW YOU SCORE WHEN YOU BEGIN EVERY SENTENCE WITH:

- "I know" **–2**
- "I feel" **+1**
- "You're right" **+2**

....

CHAPTER SUMMARY:
WHAT HAVE WE LEARNED?

- Appear to listen. And keep nodding every three seconds. That'll keep her happy.
- Your sense of humor may have been what attracted her to you in the first place. But now it just annoys her. So, please, no more impressions of Mr. Ed.
- If you are desperate for points and have no visible signs of self-respect left, then by all means, baby talk. But, please, not around the rest of us.
- Let her win the small battles. Hell, let her win the big battles, too. Practice unconditional surrender even before she draws a weapon. Then buy her a car.

....

THE SCORECARD GIFT SHOP

Here's what you get for what you did.

- You tell her that her new haircut looks great = two beers with dinner.
- You tell her it looks pretty good = Campbell's Soup for dinner.
- You engage in baby talk + in front of your best friend = she wears the stewardess outfit tonight.
- You argue with her + admit you're wrong = one rerun of "Magnum, P.I."
- You argue with her + a cheap shot about her weight = get the sheets ready for the fold-out.

4 IN THE BEDROOM (AND ELSEWHERE)

Perhaps you might pull her hair a little too hard. Or make silly animal noises during the heat of passion that all but deflate the mood. Or you may stop in the middle of hot sweaty sex only to readjust your powder wig. To you, these little indiscretions may seem inconsequential. Not to her, however. And if you continue to make the same mistakes over and over again, she will repay you in kind—by having an affair with a pool boy, a pool shark, or worse, that creepy guy in the Infiniti ads.

CREATING THE MOOD

- You prepare a romantic, candlelit dinner **0**
- oysters on the half shell **+5**
- tacos in a soft shell **−6**
- and they're still in the foil wrapper. **−15**

- You put Lou Rawls on the CD player. **+4**
- You put Twisted Sister on the CD player. **−8**
- You don't have a CD player **−15**
- but you've got a really handy Panasonic transistor radio that pulls in the local AM station. **−21**

- You light dozens of votive candles, and place them around the room +15
- in the shape of a pentagram −50
- what's with the goat? −150

- You pour her a glass of expensive champagne +6
- in a lovely crystal glass. +5
- Okay, it's not really crystal. −6
- Okay, it's not really champagne. −19

- You whip out your acoustic guitar, and play a lilting folk song that gets her all choked up +25
- and then break into a foot-stomping version of "Welcome to the Jungle." −25

- As you get ready for bed, you lift her up and carry her to the bedroom. +7
- You carry her out to the backyard −4
- to the trampoline you purchased that afternoon. −5

PREPARING YOURSELF FOR LOVE

- Before going to bed you shower and scrub in all the right places. +1
- You brush your teeth +1
- and floss them +1
- then put them back in. +5

- You put on some silk boxers. +1
- You put on some cotton sweats. −3
- You put on your crossing guard outfit. −13

- You splash on a little cologne. **+2**
- You splash on a lot of cologne. **−5**
- You're drunk on Aqua Velva. **−15**

- You suck in your gut **+½**
- You stick out your chest. **+½**
- You shave your back. **+2**
- You leave a patch that spells out "Go Eagles!" **−25**

- You blow your nose **+1**
- and swab your ears **+1**
- and check your toes for fuzz. **+1**
- You do this in the bathroom. **+2**
- You do this in bed **−5**
- while you're on top of her. **−33**

- You take off your socks. **+2**
- You put on your night-vision goggles. **−10**

LOCATION, LOCATION, LOCATION

How you score when you have sex:

- on your bed **0**
- on someone else's bed **+2**
- on a bed at a furniture showroom **−5**

- on a HealthRider **+4**
- on a Nordic Track **−4**
- while she's trying to use it **−15**

- on the hood of a parked car **+5**
- on the hood of a moving car **–5**
- on the hood of a bumper car **–20**
- in the backseat of a car **+2**
- in the front seat of a car **+1**
- with her head resting on the floor mats **–4**

- in a bathtub **+6**
- on the bathroom floor **+1**
- at the local bus station **–15**

- on top of the washing machine **+6**
- while it's on **+7**
- at the appliance store **–13**

- in a 747 **+10**
- during turbulence **+15**
- while it's taxiing **–20**

- on the beach **+15**
- in the ocean **+20**
- in the undertow **–150**

- in a swimming pool **+15**
- at the YMCA **–5**
- during Senior Aquarobics class **–20**

THE TELEVISION FACTOR

- As you and your mate get ready for sex, slowly undressing and gently touching each other, you turn off the television. **+4**

- You turn on the television. −**12**
- You channel surf with your left hand while removing her bra with your right. −**25**

THE ACT

- While making love, you tell her that you love her. +**10**
- While making love, you ask her to talk like a Swedish flight attendant. −**5**
- While making love, you start talking like a Swedish flight attendant. −**45**

- While making love you think of arcane baseball statistics to prolong your sexual stamina. +**2**
- Instead you think of the joke you heard at work and you can't help but giggle. −**30**
- You can't stop giggling. −**40**
- She starts weeping. −**60**

- When it's over, you tell her that you love her +**10**
- and you hold her in your arms all night. +**30**
- When it's over, you pat her on the butt −**10**
- and say, "Once more, for a Michelob Lite?" −**100**

- As you make love, you check yourself out in the mirror. **0**
- She catches you. −**10**
- You're giving yourself a "thumbs-up." −**34**

GENTLE SUGGESTIONS

- As you lie in bed preparing to make love, you ask her if she still has her cheerleading outfit leftover from college. **0**

- You ask her if it might be kind of fun to wear it during sex. **+1**
- She says, yes, it would be fun to wear it during sex. **+3**
- So you put it on. **–30**

YOUR REALLY STUPID SUGGESTIONS

- you suggest a threesome **–100**
- two girls (one of them is her) **–140**
- two girls (one of them is her close friend) and you **–200**
- you, an old pal, and her **–300**
- two guys and her, while you're out catching a Bears game **–300**
- you and two girls, she's not included **–574**
- you, her, and a guy dressed up as Barney **–780**
- Barney Fife **–800**

PATIENCE MY SON, PATIENCE

- Before she disrobes, you wait patiently while she gets ready for bed, as you fluff up the pillows and check yourself out in the mirror. **+1**
- Before she disrobes, you are already naked, trying to jerk her sweater over her head **–6**
- and then you make love **+5**
- while she still has the sweater up over her head. **–15**

- As the passion unfolds, you take care to remove her underwear slowly and with great care. **+3**
- In a mad rush, you give her a wedgie. **–3**
- She kinda liked it. **+4**

- You give her a hickey. **−3**
- You give her herpes. **−30**

THE FINE ART OF BIRTH CONTROL

- You take full responsibility for birth control. **+5**
- You take partial responsibility for birth control. **+2**
- Your idea of birth control is aiming for the curtains. **−10**

- You use a condom **+6**
- but only for balloon tricks. **−6**
- You're especially proud of your woolly mammoth. **−40**

- You purchase condoms on a regular basis. **+5**
- They are expensive condoms with special doodads to enhance her pleasure. **+6**
- They are cheap condoms you purchase from the dispensers in gas station bathrooms. **−7**
- They glow in the dark. **−10**
- They're not supposed to. **−50**

- Whenever a condom breaks you always let her know and then put on another one. **+5**
- Whenever a condom breaks you overlook it and only tell her afterward **−10**
- in the waiting room three months later **−30**

- Before making love, as she goes to retrieve her diaphragm, you dim the lights and put on soft music. **+5**
- While she retrieves her diaphragm, you turn on the camcorder and adjust the full length mirror. **−10**

SIMPLE STUFF

- succulent, soulful kissing **+3**
- excessive slobber **–3**

- blowing in her ear **+5**
- blowing in her nose **–4**
- blowing up the doll **–18**

- jetting your tongue gently in and out of her ear **+6**
- jetting your tongue gently in and out of her nose **–5**

- kissing her bellybutton **+4**
- removing lint with your teeth **–5**
- commenting on the taste **–25**

- slow, methodical caresses **+5**
- squeezing her breasts as if they're Nerf balls **–5**

- extended cuddling before making love **+7**
- extended cuddling after making love **+10**
- extended gas, before and after making love **–10**

- during sex, taking a breather **–15**
- during sex, taking a nap **–19**
- during sex, taking her pulse **–44**

- during sex, stopping to answer the phone **–22**
- and talking for fifteen minutes **–30**
- but not before accepting the charges **–50**

- you make love on clean sheets **+5**
- you make love on dirty sheets **–5**
- sheets with *Star Wars* characters on them **–6**

- you rip her blouse off in a passionate manner **+7**
- and then lose interest **–14**
- in line at the supermarket **–67**

- you offer cunnilingus **+10**
- you plead for fellatio **–15**
- at Burger King **–45**

- She asks you to tie her up **+5**
- so you tie her up **+6**
- and leave for the weekend **–190**

- you engage in fun, light fetishes **+4**
- you initiate some innocuous bondage **+2**
- using soft scarves **+2**
- using a blindfold **+3**
- using duct tape **–10**
- and a sawhorse **–15**

- you bring recreational sex toys to bed **+3**
- vibrators **+4**
- nicely scented oils **+5**
- a Polaroid camera **–1**
- a stuffed animal **–100**
- a real animal **–400**
- a cutout of Pamela Anderson Lee **–500**

- You bring different foods to bed as an erotic device **+5**
- like strawberries **+1**
- and whipped cream **+2**
- and a large pizza **−5**
- with extra onions **−10**

SEXY NIGHTTIME WEAR

- snug boxer-style briefs **+4**
- silk pajamas **+4**
- a scary thong **−2**
- baggy sweats **−8**
- Lycra shorts **−10**
- a storm trooper outfit **−45**

THE MASSAGE

The problem with massage: women enjoy it immensely, but only if there is no promise of sex to follow. Hint at any copulation and you kill all chances for it to occur.

- You give her a long, elaborate foot massage, gently pressing and stretching every toe **+5**
- even the toes with corns. **+7**

- You give her a long, seemingly endless back rub, to a point where she's almost in a trance. **+15**
- You touch her breasts. **−15**

- When you give her a back rub, she gently falls off to sleep. **+15**
- As she sleeps, you turn out the lights and go to bed. **+20**
- She wakes up as you're peeking under her nightgown **–20**
- with a camera. **–450**

....

CHAPTER SUMMARY:
WHAT HAVE WE LEARNED?

- Women are highly selective, in that they prefer to have sex with men who practice proper hygiene.
- Men are less selective, in that they prefer to have sex with women who will have sex with them.

....

THE SCORECARD GIFT SHOP

Here's what you get for what you did.

- Take a shower + put on aftershave + suck in the gut = oral sex.
- Engage in thirty minutes of foreplay + twenty minutes of sex + on clean sheets = you get to order pizza afterward
- A long back rub + in a room filled with lit candles + soft music = smoke a cigar inside the house.

5 FINALITY

You are about to get married. There are rings to be purchased, tuxedos to rent, and relatives to sedate. Your handy sidekick through all this, of course, is The Scorecard. One simple rule prior to the big day: Give in to every whim. Not only will it make her happy, it'll be great practice for marriage.

....

REASONS YOU GIVE HER
FOR GETTING MARRIED

- You love her dearly. **+10**
- You aren't getting any younger. **−5**
- She isn't getting any younger. **−35**
- You could use the tax break. **−60**

- You want to spend the rest of your life with her. **+25**
- You want to move out of the attic of your folks' house. **−15**
- Her parents found the home pregnancy test. **−45**
- In her lunch box. **−375**

- You say you cannot live without her for one more moment. **+45**
- You tell her it's just until you get your citizenship. **−45**

THE PROPOSAL

- You have her sit down in a quiet, romantic place **+2**
- at the upper reserved section at the Meadowlands. **−5**
- Hey—it's the playoffs! **−15**

- You kneel in front of her, and smile. **+3**
- You're kneeling on her toes. **−2**

- You pull out of your pocket a stunningly beautiful ring with a single large diamond. **+40**
- It is a modest although tasteful ring with a series of small diamonds. **+20**
- You brag about how you got it wholesale through a friend in the jewelry business. **−19**
- You overlook removing the finger of the previous owner. **−275**

- You propose to her in a romantic and very expensive restaurant **+10**
- accompanied by a violinist **+15**
- and a pre-nup agreement. **−130**

- You propose to her using a skywriter **+15**
- "Dori wll u narry m e luv Roberr" **−4**

- You propose to her using a singing telegram. **+3**
- "Hey honey, let's give it a shot! We'll save on rent if we tie the knot!" **−15**

- You propose to her using Federal Express **−5**
- that's because of the restraining order. **−40**

....

THE ART OF INTRODUCTIONS

The developing status of your relationship must be publicized. Underplay the relationship, and you're dead meat.

- At a party, you introduce her affectionately as your fiancée followed by her first name only. **+1**
- When you introduce her, you neglect to mention she's your fiancée. **−10**
- Especially when you're talking to other available women. **−20**
- Then she becomes, "Uh . . . my girlfriend." **−15**
- You don't mention she's your fiancée until she elbows you in the side **−9**
- and then you always add, "But we haven't really set a date." **−50**

....

THE BACHELOR PARTY

This rite of a passage can be a lot of fun for everyone involved. But sadly, many bachelor parties have also proved to be horrendous disasters. Just ask any Kennedy.

- Your pals throw you a bachelor party. **−10**
- It's a wild bachelor party complete with cigars and booze **−25**

- and strippers. **−78**
- Is that Charlie Sheen? **−125**

- Your friends hire an "exotic dancer" from a reputable company they found in the Yellow Pages. **−30**
- They hire a stripper on a quick drive through the seamier part of town. **−60**
- She's quite a husky girl. **−65**
- You realize when she gets naked, she's not a girl at all. **−135**
- But did that stop you? **−270**

- There are numerous strippers at the party. **−150**
- There are handcuffs involved. **−160**
- Someone brought a donkey. **−220**
- That someone was Jimmy Swaggart. **−245**

- Your bachelor party is a quaint affair at a small restaurant, where everyone makes speeches and wishes you the best of luck. **+2**
- There are no strippers. **+6**
- There are no drinking games. **+5**
- There is no donkey. **+10**
- You don't even get drunk. **+15**
- It doesn't matter, and lying just makes it worse. **−100**

HER FAMILY

When you get married, you aren't just acquiring a wife. You are also acquiring a whole set of strangers: a cranky elderly couple, a few twisted siblings, a strange uncle and an aunt with a bushier mustache than Gene Shalit.

But get them to accept you—hell, even to like you—then you can earn major points. Even better, if her family comes to adore you, it means more than just free meals. We're talking easy, low-interest loans.

- You visit her parents regularly. **+2**
- You visit her parents, and actually make pleasant conversation. **+3**
- You visit her parents regularly, and spend most of your time staring vacantly at the television **–3**
- and the television is off **–6**
- and so is your shirt. **–15**

- When you visit you are always well dressed, wearing a V-neck sweater, khakis, and loafers. **+1**
- When you visit you are always wearing cut-offs and an Ozzy Osbourne T-shirt. **–5**.
- And a really big, shiny Confederate flag belt buckle. **–8**
- You won it in a knife fight, you tell everyone proudly. **–16**

- You call her dad "Sir." **+5**
- You call him by his first name. **0**
- You call him "Pops." **–8**
- You call him "old man." **–15**
- You call him "old fart." **–65**

- You always bring gifts to the house when you visit: **+2**
- a basket of fruit for the family **+2**
- a handful of nice cigars for Dad **+3**
- a bouquet of flowers for Mom **+4**
- a six-pack for your mate's deadbeat brother **–5**
- a wad of cash for her little sister **–9**
- who still has the Polaroids **–50**

- You're always willing to help out with the small chores around their house: **+5**
- you help Mom clean the kitchen and do the dishes **+5**
- you help Pop build a fire in the fireplace **+5**
- you help bro with his geometry homework **+5**
- you help sis off with her clothes. **−14**

- When your mother-in-law offers you some of her "famous" head cheese popovers, you accept them. **+11**
- You eat one without gagging or vomiting. **+2**
- You eat two. **+4**
- You're actually dumping them behind the sofa **−5**
- The dog finds them **−15**
- and he gags and vomits. **−20**
- The mother recognizes her popovers. **−30**

- You send a holiday wreath to her mother. **+10**
- You send her father tickets to a ball game. **+10**
- You drop by the house just to say hello to her mother, even when your mate isn't around. **+10**
- You make yourself at home, and stay, even after everyone else goes out **−20**
- except the sister. **−30**

- You're always willing to indulge the father in any of his quirky or boring hobbies. **+5**
- You act interested when he shows you his elaborate train set in the basement. **+7**
- You are fascinated by his collection of commemorative presidential plates from the Franklin Mint. **+10**
- You are frightened by his large stockpile of Nazi war memorabilia. **−15**

- You never get drunk in front of her parents. **+3**
- Actually, you can't remember if you do or don't. **–30**

You always leave their house:
- with a pan of leftovers and a hearty hug from the parents **+7**
- when the patrolman instructs you to **–15**

....

TYING THE KNOT

Yes, the wedding ceremony is a truly beautiful spectacle. But one mistake and you'll be cleaning the gutters for the rest of your life. So remember this: even though both of you are getting married—it's her wedding, not yours.

- When your fiancée informs you that she wants the wedding to be a large, glorious affair at the most expensive hotel in the city, you say, "Sounds great, Luv." **+5**
- When she explains how she'd like only the finest silver and china place settings, you suggest that maybe a fully stocked bar might be a better investment. **–6**
- When she mentions that she'd really like engraved invitations, with raised print on the envelope, you suggest that maybe a fully stocked bar might be a better investment. **–10**
- When she asks you if you still want to get married, you suggest that maybe a fully stocked bar might be a better investment. **–120**

THE GUEST LIST

- You realize that both of you have exceeded the limit for guests, so you suggest that both of you start removing names from your respective lists, until you pare it down to an ideal number. **−20**

- You suggest that you start removing names from your list only until number is within the limit. **+5**
- As it turns out the only people you end up inviting are your parents. **+6**
- Meanwhile she invites her homeroom teacher from junior high. **+5**
- And some woman she met in line at the drugstore. **+9**
- And Antonio Banderas. **+10**

THE CEREMONY

- When the minister asks if you take her to be your wife, you say "I do" emphatically. **+10**
- You ask him to repeat the question. **−90**

- When the minister says, "You may now kiss the bride," you give her a long, passionate but wholesome smooch **+3**
- which smudges her bridal makeup. **−35**

- You give her a nice peck on the lips. **+4**
- You french-kiss her **−5**
- and grab her butt. **−16**

THE RECEPTION

- During the reception, you have a few glasses of champagne, but remain cordial and coherent throughout. **+5**
- During the reception, you have seventeen glasses of champagne, and return to the hotel with a bridesmaid's phone number written on your hand. **−25**
- Well, maybe not your hand. **−89**

THE HONEYMOON

- You devote a lot of time and effort to selecting the honeymoon destination together. **+3**
- You let her pick the honeymoon destination. **+9**
- Heck, you always wanted to see the birthplace of Louisa May Alcott. **+15**

- When packing for the honeymoon, you manage to fit everything you need in one suitcase and a grip. **+3**
- You happily carry her six suitcases and two small carry-ons **+5**
- as well as her parakeet. **+34**

- When you're limited for luggage space, you leave your suitcase behind. **+5**
- You didn't need your insulin anyway. **+18**

As your honeymoon destination you choose to:
- go on a three-week jaunt through the best hotels in Europe **+15**
- spend ten days in Hawaii, wearing baggy shorts and drinking frozen cocktails **+6**
- rough it for a week in a rustic cabin in the woods **+2**
- where some strange bald-headed guys play banjos next door. **−30**
- You guys hit it off great. **−50**
- They're coming to visit you next summer. **−150**

CHAPTER SUMMARY:
WHAT HAVE WE LEARNED?

- Don't propose to her in a casual manner. Have your secretary do it.
- When getting to know her family, stay out of the liquor cabinet and the sister's drawers.
- Try to avoid getting involved in any of the wedding preparations. Your only responsibility is to show up on time for the ceremony. And don't bring a date.
- The honeymoon is neither the time or place to discuss seeing other people. Wait a few months. Then spring it on her.

THE SCORECARD GIFT SHOP

Here's what you get for what you did.

- You propose to her on bended knee + huge rock for her finger = a bachelor party.
- One big bachelor party = three weeks of suspicious looks.
- Visit her parents + make polite conversation with them = eighteen holes of golf with Rick the fat guy from work.
- Visit her parents for dinner + help do the dishes = argument on the drive home on why you never do the dishes at home.
- Get really drunk at the wedding reception = lots of free time during the honeymoon.

6 THE DUTIES OF MARRIAGE

Many relationship experts and marriage counselors will tell you that marriage is a 50/50 partnership. You do things for your mate, and she does the same for you.

God love 'em, but these folks are clearly living in a dream world.

••

GIVING UP STUFF

A woman measures the depth of your love not by your romantic gestures or physical affection, but by the number of insidious habits you're willing to sacrifice for her. The more you cherished these practices when you were single, the more points you get when you give them up. And, by the way, promiscuity doesn't count.

- You give up smoking cigars. **+10**
- You give up smoking cigarettes. **+15**
- You give up smoking crack. **+20**

- You give up hanging out at bars. **+15**
- You give up sleeping in bars. **+20**
- You give up sleeping with bartenders. **+45**

- You give up your habitual weekend drinking binges. **+15**
- You give up the apartment you share with Mickey Rourke. **+30**

- You give up wearing baseball caps and sweats when shopping. **+2**
- You give up wearing baseball caps and sweats to bed. **+5**
- You give up wearing the clown outfit to family gatherings. **+6**

- You give up fast food. **+5**
- You give up junk food. **+9**
- You give up all the food you used to enjoy. **+20**
- Like meat, cheese, eggs, and dairy products. **+25**

- You give up playing guitar in a band. **+6**
- The band was Pearl Jam. **+18**

You give up a hobby that is dear to you:
- fly-fishing **+4**
- bowling **+6**
- stamp collecting **+8**
- gambling **+12**
- armed robbery **+15**
- modern dance **+20**
- performing comedy at open mike nights **+30**

- You give up your pristine 1969 Corvette, the same one you've tinkered with since you were in high school. **+24**

- You give up your pristine 1974 AMC Gremlin, the same one you've tinkered with since you were in high school. **+44**
- It had a really "bitchin" sound system, too. **+50**

- You give up a great job in another part of the country to accommodate her career plans. **+30**
- She sells Mary Kay cosmetics. **+35**

Then, of course, there are things you used to do prior to marriage that she loved, which you no longer do since you've tied the knot. Don't think for a minute she hasn't noticed.

- You no longer buy her flowers. **−15**
- You no longer buy her chocolates. **−20**
- You no longer buy her sexy underthings out of the blue. **−30**
- You no longer buy her anything. **−134**
- Well, except for the membership to Weight Watchers. **−250**

- You no longer hold her hand. **−20**
- You no longer hold her place in line. **−22**
- You no longer hold back your gas. **−55**

- You no longer have morning sex. **−24**
- You no longer have lunchtime sex. **−29**
- You no longer have evening sex. **−60**
- You no longer have sex in unusual places **−30**
- like, say, the bed. **−35**

- You no longer talk in baby talk. **−40**
- You no longer talk at all. **−50**
- Except for "pass the ketchup." **−75**

- You no longer compliment her on her beauty **–45**
- or her figure **–50**
- or her new boyfriend. **–55**

- You no longer call her "Snookums." **–40**
- You no longer call her anything **–50**
- except "hey you." **–75**

··

YOUR CHILDREN

You might think it's a bit cynical to exploit your offspring for scoring big points, but hey, it's better than using them as throw pillows.

- When the baby cries, you get out of bed to see what's wrong. **+2**
- When the baby cries, you fake like you're asleep. **–3**
- When the baby cries, you say to your mate, "I believe that popped out of you." **–7**

- You share responsibilities in changing diapers. **+3**
- You change the baby's diapers more than she does. **+8**
- You have never seen a diaper up close in your life. **–5**
- Well, except for the one you wear now and then. **–30**

- You feed the baby **+4**
- those little jars of baby food **+1**
- beer nuts and soda pop **–15**
- or whatever you can find under the cushions of the couch. **–30**

- You love to film your children with the camcorder **+7**
- so much so, they've never seen the right side of your face. **–14**

- You read to your children before they fall asleep. **+5**
- From a book of imaginative fairy tales **+6**
- From a book of Bible stories **+7**
- from the sports pages **–5**
- from *Penthouse* "Letters" **–30**
- from your entry in *Penthouse* "Letters." **–50**

- You spend a lot of time with your kids **+34**
- from previous marriages. **–40**

- You don't spend any time with your own kids. **–50**
- They don't seem to mind. **–75**

- You buy your children educational toys to encourage the learning process **+7**
- and you end up playing with them more than they do. **–5**

- You buy your kids well-armed action figures designed to kill other well-armed action figures **–9**
- and you end up playing with them more than they do. **–20**

- You limit their television viewing hours to only wholesome fare. **+10**
- You limit their television viewing to every waking hour. **–10**

- You used to let them watch Sam Donaldson regularly. **–120**
- They still get nightmares over his hair. **–140**

- You help them with their homework. **+15**
- You do their homework **–15**
- and they still get D's. **–30**

- You watch the kids so your wife can have some fun one night. **+15**
- You watch the kids so your wife can have some fun one night, and you fall asleep on watch. **–10**
- You wake up to find the car missing **–40**
- as well as your hunting rifle and ski masks. **–50**

- When the time is right, you teach them the birds and bees. **+15**
- When the time is right, you let them watch the Playboy Channel **–15**
- and they learn more about sex than you ever did. **–30**

- You drive your kids to school in the morning. **+5**
- You pick them up from soccer or band practice **+7**
- and drive them home **+9**
- but not before stopping at Hooters for a shot and a beer. **–20**

- You buy your teenage kids beer. **–50**
- You don't buy your teenage kids beer **0**
- not since you got them fake I.D.'s for their birthdays. **–90**

- You try to act like your kids. **–5**
- You use their lingo ("cool," "rad," "ragin'") **–10**
- You listen to their music and dress like them. **–20**
- You have a paper route. **–130**
- And a bike with a banana seat. **–145**

A NIGHT OUT, JUST THE TWO OF YOU

Life is a lot different now that you've been together as husband and wife. Things are no longer wildly spontaneous. You have responsibilities. She has responsibilities. So when you finally have an opportunity to have some fun together without the kids or the job hanging over your head, you'd better make it work. Two quick pointers: find a good baby-sitter, and then take a shower. And no, not with the baby-sitter.

GOING TO THE MOVIES

- You take her to a movie. **+2**
- You take her to a movie she likes. **+4**
- You take her to a movie she'll like that you'll hate. **+6**
- It's one of those foreign films. **+10**
- This movie is three hours long **+8**
- with subtitles. **+9**
- The plot concerns a group of seamstresses who tell stories to each other while they work. **+10**
- The stories are mostly about how rotten men are. **+15**
- There is no sex or violence in this movie **+16**
- but there is a lot of crying **+17**
- some of it, strangely, is coming from you. **−10**

- You even pretend to enjoy the movie, holding her hand during weepy parts. **+35**
- Okay, maybe not her hand. **−10**

- You decide to get frisky. **−3**
- You do this during the climactic scene where the heroine is executed by a band of angry misogynists **−12**

- and you've got your hand down your mate's blouse. **−12**
- That's not your hand. **−34**
- That's not your mate. **−40**

- You convince your mate to see a movie you'll like. **−2**
- It's called *Savage Rototiller.* **−7**
- You tell her it's about a love affair between two archaeologists, set in the early 1800s. **+2**
- You lied. It's actually about a mad gardener who systematically kills young nubile cheerleaders with a lethal Rototiller **−15**
- but there's a subplot involving azaleas. **+2**

- After the first massacre, she gets up and walks out. **−15**.
- You get up and walk out, too. **0**
- To get more Raisinets. **−60**

GOING TO A CLUB

- You take her to a club. **0**
- It's hip, hot and has a bouncer. **+5**
- Inside, the featured act is an angry female folk singer **+10**
- who obviously has a thing against men **+13**
- even though she kind of looks like one. **+13**.
- You sit through the act, and even pretend to be moved by the music. **+25**
- You even sway your head back and forth to the beat. **+27**
- You fake a good cry. **+30**
- You buy this folk singer's CD **+33**
- and play it now and then just to look sensitive. **+35**
- You tell your mate how much you admire this folk singer **+10**
- because she's got a better looking girlfriend than you. **−25**

GOING TO A COMEDY CLUB

- You go to see a comic. **+2**
- The comic is female. **+3**
- Her entire routine is about the constant hilarity of premenstrual syndrome **+5**
- and you laugh along, even though she's not funny **+6**
- because she's got a great rack. **–5**

- You go to see a comic, and it's a guy. **+1**
- He's crude and sexist. **–2**
- You laugh. **–5**
- You don't laugh at all. In fact, you stifle even the slightest chuckle, and look seriously offended throughout. **+2**
- No, you laugh. **–5**
- You laugh too much. **–10**
- Your mate isn't laughing. **–15**
- You laugh harder. **–25**
- She doesn't say a thing during the ride home **–30**
- because she's busy humming "I Am Woman." **–40**

··

TRIPS TO THE MALL

In case you haven't noticed, the mall is not a man's place. How so?

There are no hardware stores or bars in a shopping mall.

THE TRIP

- You go to the mall together on a Saturday afternoon. **+3**
- You go to the mall together, at its busiest time **+1**

- You go to the mall together, even though there's a great Clint Eastwood movie on TV. **+4**
- One that doesn't star an orangutan. **+6**

- You go to the mall together, even though Dallas is playing Chicago for the play-off. **+6**
- You go to the mall together, even though you're sick with the flu. **+6**
- No, make that malaria. **+9**
- That doesn't matter because it's a giant red-tag sale. **+5**
- You ask your wife why she wants to buy a whole bunch of giant red tags. **–10**

- You drive to the mall, drop her off at the entrance, then park the car. **+6**
- You drive to the mall, drop her off at the entrance, then head to a sports bar to catch the Dallas/49ers play-off game before it's too late. **–4**
- The game goes into overtime. **–10**
- You forget to pick her up **–30**
- but you eventually remember, at work, the next day. **–233**

THE WOMAN'S DEPARTMENT

- You go to the mall with her and you accompany her to the woman's apparel section of a large department store. **0**
- You sit down in a nearby chair and wait patiently as she tries many things on. **+2**
- You keep busy by counting to one million by threes. **+8**
- You make it to 976,830. **+10**
- Every now and then she comes out in a new outfit, and you give her positive, constructive criticism. **+3**

- She can't find you because you've hidden in a crawlspace with the teenaged salesclerk. **–100**
- That's okay because your mate still has your credit cards. **+20**

THE LINGERIE SHOP

- You enter a lingerie shop. **+1**
- You enter a lingerie shop without ogling or touching the mannequins. **+2**
- You brush up against a mannequin. **–5**
- A part comes off in your hand. **–15**
- You take it home with you. **–20**
- You sleep with it. **–120**

- You ask the buxom salesgirl if she might locate some satin teddies for your mate. **+6**
- You ask the buxom salesgirl if she wouldn't mind modeling them for you **–25**
- at a local motel. **–75**

THE POTPOURRI EXPERIENCE

- She visits a potpourri shop, and you follow. **0**
- She visits a potpourri shop, and you *want* to follow. **+2**
- You find a candle that's shaped like a unicorn. **+5**
- You decide you will buy this unicorn-shaped candle. **+10**
- It will make a great back-scratcher. **–6**

- You pick up some really tantalizing chocolates. **0**
- You grab one and eat it. **–15**
- It's designer soap. **–20**
- It tastes pretty good. **–35**

HOW FAR WILL YOU TRAVEL TO A MALL?

The farther you'll go the more you'll get, pointwise.

- Two miles. **0**
- To the next town, fifteen miles away. **+1**
- To the next county, forty-five miles away. **+6**
- Across state lines, four hours away. **+20**
- You've booked a flight. **+30**

SOCIAL ENGAGEMENTS

Don't be fooled, my friend, for parties and get-togethers are minefields of monstrous proportions. There are many, many opportunities for you to say something inappropriate, do something foolish, knock something over, or kiss someone or something right on the lips who isn't your date. And that's while you're hanging your coat.

That's why you need to spend extra time assessing your behavior. The fact is, your relationship, like a stuffed bear, is on public display for all to poke and prod. Worse, if there are any unhappy couples in the vicinity, you can bet they'll take special pleasure in seeing your relationship run aground as well. It makes them feel less miserable. Your mate is aware of that and you need to be, too.

MAKING AN ENTRANCE

- You arrive at the party, bearing a bottle of wine for the hosts. **0**
- You arrive at the party, bearing a bottle of something the hosts had given to you at your party last year. **−4**
- It's already been opened. **−12**
- Hey—it had a screw top! **−20**

- You arrive at the party, dressed appropriately, looking polished and professional. **+5**
- You arrive at the party, hopelessly underdressed and reeking of cigarette smoke **−4**
- and wearing a baseball cap with a dumb saying on it. **−5**
- "Gone fishin'." **−6**

MINGLING

- Once safely inside the affair, you stay by your mate's side during the entire party. **0**
- Your hand never leaves the small of her back **+3**
- as you guide her from guest to guest, engaging in warm conversation with all those around you. **+5**
- You stay by her side for a while, but then stray from her side once you spy an old drinking buddy from college. **−6**
- That old drinking buddy is named Heather. **−8**
- Heather got implants. **−10**
- But they certainly feel real. **−120**

- As you mingle among the guests, you make sure to hold your mate's hand, and shoot her adoring glances every minute or so. **+2**

- As you mingle among the guests, you introduce her jokingly as "my first wife." **−10**
- You follow this with a swift, loud, but affectionate pat on the rump. **−20**

- When your mate points to a sexy woman in a skimpy black skirt and asks you if you find her attractive, you reply with the utmost sincerity: "Yes, but nowhere near as attractive as you." **+3**
- When your mate points to a woman in a skimpy black skirt and asks you if you think she is attractive, you say, "Yeah, but don't worry, she's terrible in bed." **−25**
- That woman is her sister. **−75**

- At the party you have one drink, then cut yourself off and start drinking Evian **0**
- because you're the designated driver **+3**
- and the amphetamines are kicking in. **−24**

- At the party, she gets embarrassingly drunk and you stay sober. **+5**
- You end up being the responsible one, escorting her out and getting her home safely **+15**
- and you brag about it for weeks. **−10**

- At the party, you have more than one drink, and that's it. **0**
- You have more than a few drinks and perform the macarena with a large poodle. **−12**
- You have a lot of drinks and vaguely remember being finger-printed. **−34**

ON PROPERLY GREETING HER BOSS
AT HER HOLIDAY OFFICE PARTY

- "It's nice to meet you, I've heard a lot of good things about you." **+2**
- "Hey, you're not so fat!" **−30**
- "So, how's AA going?" **−45**

THE PROPER EXIT.

- You always leave well before the party ends. **+6**
- You're always the last to leave **−5**
- and your mate has to drag you out by your belt buckle **−6**
- which means you still have your pants on. **+4**

....

ACTS OF HEROISM

These days, it still pays to be chivalrous. Especially when there are points at stake.

PROWLERS

- You check out a suspicious noise at night. **0**
- You check out a suspicious noise at night and it's nothing. **0**
- You check out a suspicious noise at night and it's something. **+5**
- Whatever it is, you smack it with a six iron. **+10**
- It's her disoriented grandfather. **−10**

CONFRONTING A MUGGER

- When leaving a restaurant late at night, the two of you are confronted by a mugger, and you:

- instruct your mate to hand over her purse, as you hand over your watch and wallet **0**
- foil the mugger with a swift punch that knocks him unconscious **+20**
- use her as a shield **−100**

CONFRONTING A BAD WAITER

- A waiter has been giving you and your mate consistently rotten service all night, and she urges you to do something about it. **−5**
- You order dessert. **−15**

FAMILY EMERGENCIES

- The fire alarm goes off at 3 A.M. and you get up to check for smoke. **0**
- You find a smoldering fire in the kitchen, and race back to the bedroom to rescue your mate. **+5**
- You find a smoldering fire in the kitchen, and you successfully smother the flames **+50**
- with her cat. **−100**

- You rouse your mate and carry her down the stairs to safety. **+20**
- But not before rescuing the television. **−100**
- It's cable-ready! **−200**

....

WHEN SHE'S SICK

When your mate falls ill, it offers ample opportunity to earn a welcome wagon of points. Tend to her every need, and you can achieve sainthood in just days.

- She has the flu, and you cater to her every need. **+5**
- You drive to the only twenty-four-hour pharmacy in town, at 3 A.M., to pick up decongestant **+7**
- and some Vicks **+2**
- and a humidifier **+5**
- and as long as you're out, some hairspray and nail polish **+16**
- and some Saran Wrap ("It's on sale!!!") **+17**

- You bring her some soup **+10**
- not from a can, but from a gourmet deli from across town. **+15**
- You stop for a beer on the way home and the soup gets cold. **−15**
- You tell her its gazpacho. **−20**

- You bring her magazines to read in bed. **+5**
- These are magazines no man should ever purchase in public **+8**
- like tabloids, soap opera reviews, astrology monthlies, *Us* magazine. **+11**
- You end up reading them. **−9**
- And doing the self-quizzes. **−18**
- And flunking. **−40**

- You fluff up her pillows **+4**
- apply cold compresses to her head **+4**

- pump her full of medication **+4**
- until she's fast asleep **+4**
- she wakes up a month later **–145**
- in Pakistan **–779**

....

HER NIGHT OUT

Rejoice! By all means let her go if she asks. By granting her free-dom, she should hopefully give you some in return. Especially if she has a really, really good time, and as a result, gets sick all over the driveway.

- You watch the kids while she goes out with her annoying work friends **+5**
- She goes out with her annoying work friends and she comes home late **+10**
- from one of those all-male strip clubs. **+16**
- She's very drunk on big fruity drinks. **+20**
- She's got a thong in her pocket **+25**
- and a phone number written on her forearm. **+30**

- She comes home late and drunk on big fruity drinks and you gently put her to bed. **+33**
- She comes home late and drunk on big fruity drinks and you gently put her to bed, but not before she pukes **+35**
- in the bathroom **+35**
- in the bedroom **+40**
- in the driveway, in front of the neighbors **+50**
- which you clean up **+65**
- and brag about for weeks. **–45**

....

A NIGHT OUT WITH YOUR PALS

You may look at this as fun. But remember, just by leaving the house, you've already lost points in her eyes. So make it worthwhile: Do not spend the evening shopping for floor mats for your AMC Pacer.

- You meet a buddy at a sports bar **–5**
- and the buddy is married **–4**
- happily married **–3**
- and bald, too. **0**
- And your mate knows his wife. **+1**

- You meet a buddy who is single. **–10**
- He is frighteningly single **–15**
- and he drives a Trans Am. **–17**
- It is a Trans Am with a personalized license plate **–20**
- 1 GR8 FK **–26**

- You have a few beers with this single buddy **–22** (For every beer after three, subtract two extra points.)
- and miss curfew by an hour **–30**
- By three hours. **–50**
- You get home at 4 A.M. smelling of booze and cigars **–70**
- and perfume. **–90**
- And the perfume is better than the stuff your mate wears **–100**
- and you're not wearing any pants. **–150**
- Is that a tattoo? **–200**

....

FUNERALS

One of the problems men have as a group is that we usually see every kind of gathering—no matter the occasion—as an opportunity for free food. This is a problem at funerals.

- You show up on time at the church, wearing a somber suit. **0**
- You show up on time at the church, dressed in khakis, polo shirt, and loafers. **–15**
- When she asks you why you're dressed like that, you say, "Hey—it's not my uncle!" **–30**

- During the funeral, you stand quietly, and hold your mate while she weeps to herself. **+4**
- Meanwhile, you're glancing at your Sony Watchman (there's no sense compounding the misery by missing the Bulls). **–15**

- When it comes time to pay your last respects, you walk up to the casket, say a brief prayer, and walk away. **+1**
- You stare down at the corpse and say, "Is that a Hugo Boss?" **–20**

- When you talk to the bereaved, you offer your sincerest condolences. **+3**
- When you talk to the bereaved, you mention that the departed and you had a lot in common **+3**
- including chest size. **–6**
- "If you weren't doing anything with his ski jackets . . ." **–24**

··

THE VACATION

Any mistake or blunder is amplified when you're traveling. You'll figure this out the moment you return and she tells you not to bother unpacking.

- You convince her that you both need to really get away. **+3**
- Separately. **−40**
- She asks you where you'd like to go on vacation and you don't say, "Wherever you'd like dear." **−5**
- You actually suggest some places you'd like to go on this vacation. **−2**
- Each place you choose has an uncanny proximity to:
- casinos **−5**
- horse racing tracks **−8**
- strip joints **−10**
- your ex-girlfriend's condo. **−45**
- You nod politely to all her suggestions, none of which interest you: **−3**
- her parents house in the Catskills **+15**
- her aunt's house in central Pennsylvania **+20**
- her sister's trailer home in Florida **+20**
- a New Age spa featuring mud baths and seaweed wraps. **+34**
- You bring a Game Boy. **−70**

- You and her finally settle on some exotic place you can't pronounce. **+10**
- It's an island. **+15**
- The airport runway is a pineapple field. **−10**

- You look through the brochures, and show her a hotel you think best fits your budget.

- It is a luxury hotel right on the beach, complete with pool bars, nightly entertainment, a gym, masseur, and several five-star restaurants. **+15**
- It is a collection of quaint bungalows, near the beach, with a nice view, a restaurant, and a pool. **+11**
- It is a motel lodge with a beverage and ice machine only on odd-numbered floors **–10**
- but it has cable! **–15**

- You pick up many souvenirs **+3**
- made of shellacked wood and shells **–6**
- or worse, coconuts **–15**
- postcards of naked women with sand on their butts **–45**

- On vacation, you indulge in expensive dinners, purchase pricey clothes, and take part in many exotic adventures. **+30**
- On vacation, you're amazed at how many really good movies they have on Spectravision. **–30**

- On vacation, money is no object as you lavish her with trinkets and baubles. **+30**
- On vacation, you keep running short on cash. **–15**
- Yet you keep buying drinks for drunken servicemen **–45**

- When you return from vacation, you find that you forgot to tell the paperboy to stop delivering the papers **–5**
- even though your mate had told you to do just that about a half dozen times. **–10**
- Now the papers are piled up high on your front porch **–20**
- which signaled a prowler, who cleaned out everything you owned. **–40**

- Including her collection of precious stuffed animals she's had since she was a kid. **-60**
- So the vacation wasn't an entire bust. **-10**

....

THE HOLIDAYS

If you don't fulfill your duties, you're going to find more than coal in your stocking.

- One month before Christmas, you lug the boxes full of holiday decorations down from the attic. **+5**
- One week before Christmas, you lug the boxes full of holiday decorations down from the attic. **-5**
- The night before Christmas, you lug down the boxes full of holiday decorations down from the attic. **-20**
- And pick up a tree at the local Shop Rite. **-30**
- It's half-price **-35**
- and it's made of plastic. **-50**
- White plastic. **-55**

- You put up the Christmas tree. **+1**
- It's crooked. **-4**
- You say it looks good crooked. **-12**

- You decorate the tree together. **+2**
- You hang wreaths on the door. **+1**
- You hang a wreath on every door. **+3**
- You hang a wreath on your "one-eyed friend" and invite her to smell the fresh pine scent. **-25**

- You put lights on the house. **+10**
- Half of them are out. **−10**
- You don't take them down until Easter. **−30**

- For Hannukah, you buy her a number of gifts. **+30**
- Some of them are very expensive. **+50**
- One gift is bowling shoes. **−15**
- She decides that the day after Hannukah ends she wants you to go with her to return nearly all of the gifts. **−20**
- Receipts? **−30**

CHAPTER SUMMARY: WHAT HAVE WE LEARNED?

- Anything you enjoyed doing when you were single is verboten once you're married. Especially if these endeavors involved high speed chases, packing firearms, or listening to Howard Stern.
- Children will only cost you points, unless you use them well. We hear Kathie Lee Gifford's hiring.
- Potpourri is a very good thing. Say that ten times.
- Parties require extreme caution. Stick by your wife at all times, and keep your eyes from glancing at anything with a plunging neckline. Unless it's Dennis Rodman.
- Stay away from all of your single friends, especially any of them who still have a full head of hair and drive cars with really "bitchin" sound systems.
- Never deny her a girl's night out. It can only help you in the future. Especially when she stumbles onto that secret room behind the false wall in the basement.

···

THE SCORECARD GIFT SHOP

Here's what you get for what you did.

- Shop for dishware + shop for furniture = one hour at the driving range.
- Shop for dishware + one stop at the candle store = unlimited time at the driving range.
- One stop at the candle store – you drop a ceramic unicorn on the floor = absolutely nothing.
- Take her to a horribly violent movie + hoot loudly whenever a character is decapitated by rotating blades = visit a potpourri shop afterward + purchase $50 worth of scented products.
- Go out with an old friend + come home early and sober = she makes you dinner.
- Go out with an old friend – come home without your pants = four weekends shopping for designer soaps.
- Take care of her when she's sick = you catch whatever she had.

7 BE THE MAN OF THE HOUSE (AND ELSEWHERE)

Master a few simple "guy duties" (fixing a leaky faucet, changing the car oil, chasing off a Jehovah's Witness), then you'll shine in your mate's eyes. Just clean out the bloodstains afterward.

HANDYMAN SKILLS

We live in a progressive age where most men are no longer required to wield a hammer, operate a sander, or screw in a bolt. Nowadays, that's what we pay those kids who went to junior college to do. Yet, there is still some luster attached to a tool belt. Sometimes women are more impressed by a guy who can install a window than a guy who can install Windows. Just remember this one rule: never try to hammer anything after three Old Milwaukees. At that point, start using the nail gun.

YOUR EXPERTISE

- You have a keen understanding of the various tools in your chest. **+1**

- You know what a bone wrench is. **+1**
- As well as a C-clamp, U-bolt, O-ring, S-trap and J-bend. **+3**
- and a crowfoot wrench, a gooseneck bar, a bullnose plane, and a butterfly hinge **+3**
- and a cat's paw nail puller, clamshell moulding, duckbill snips, and a plumber's snake **+3**
- Yet the house is still falling apart. **−20**

TOOLS THAT COST YOU POINTS

Please note that while owning a set of shiny tools might make you quite the handyman in your home and neighborhood, some tools—by virtue of their odd and lewd-sounding names—will cost you points. Point losses double if you ever use them in formal dinner conversation.

- You own a ballcock. **−5**
- You own a reamer. **−5**
- You own a deep throat socket. **−5**
- You bring them to parties. **−20**

And, of course, there are some tools you might own that cost you points because they're too damn big.

- You own a bulldozer. **−75**
- You park it on the lawn. **−80**
- You own a cement mixer. **−100**
- You charge neighborhood kids for "spins." **−175**

YOUR ABILITY TO FIX EVERYDAY PROBLEMS

- When the toilet is suffering from an irritating case of "endless flush," you are able to fix the problem quickly yourself. **+3**

- When the toilet is suffering from an irritating case of "endless flush," you call a plumber to come and fix it. **0**
- When the toilet is suffering from a case of "endless flush," you jiggle the lever, and go back to bed. **–5**
- And tell her to think of it like camping near a stream. **–12**

- When the toilet is clogged, and you unclog it with a handy plunger. **+5**
- When the toilet is clogged, you keep flushing it until you have to flee the overflowing wave of raw sewage. **–10**
- When the toilet is clogged, you grab whatever is handy to unclog it **–3**
- like her curling iron. **–5**
- You tell her about it months later. **–100**

- The VCR is flashing "12:00" and you reprogram it to stop. **+1**
- The VCR is flashing "12:00" and you cover it with duct tape. **–1**

- You pride yourself on your ability to put things together. **0**
- So much so you never refer to a product's instructions. **–10**
- Which could explain why the garage door crushed Fifi. **–150**

LEAKS

- You know how to fix one. **+5**
- You know how to take one. **–5**

··

MAJOR WEEKEND PROJECTS

Remember, these types of large, time-consuming projects are ideal for Saturday afternoon (provided there is nothing good on TV). A large project can offer you hours of blissful solitude, not to mention an excuse to fill up the ice chest with cheap beer.

- You tackle a large household project with élan. **+15**
- Élan is a delightful au pair you met at the mall. **–22**

- You know the drying time of a matte varnish. **+14**
- You thought matte varnish was a well-coiffed newscaster. -5

- You know the difference between hand-blocked, machine-printed, vinyl and woodchip wallpaper **+6**
- because some of each is peeling from the walls of your house. **–15**
- You prefer to call it "rustic." **–17**

- You spend a Saturday refinishing the floors. **+20**
- You spend a Saturday rewiring the basement. **+25**
- You spend a Saturday adding a second floor. **+35**
- You spend a Saturday painting a mural on the wall of the guest bedroom **+40**
- that features unicorns, cherubs, and rainbows **+45**
- that features various NFL greats. **–45**
- You spend a Saturday setting up a Nerf ball hoop over the bathroom wastebasket **–10**
- and you're organizing pick-up games. **–25**

- You like to boast that you're pretty good at fixing things **+5**
- which is your way of saying you never went to college. **–40**

THE PRICE OF HANDYMAN INJURIES

You'll find it doesn't always hurt to get hurt. In fact, injuries might even earn you points—without you having to actually finish the job!

- a swollen thumb. **0**
- a minor cut or bruise **0**
- a broken or dislocated digit **+2**
- a broken limb **+7**
- a broken limb you got from showing off **–3**
- while high up on a ladder **+2**
- okay, a step ladder. **–6**

- Falling through the roof **+34**
- And bleeding on the freshly shampooed rug. **–45**

....

GETTING YOUR HANDS DIRTY, OR HANDLING THINGS OF A DISGUSTING NATURE (INCLUDING RELIGIOUS ZEALOTS)

It is in our masculine nature to be burdened with the unsavory responsibilities of life. Anything of a disgusting nature is our turf. Anything that is grimy, slimy, or smelly and makes women run screaming invariably falls on our plates. Unless it comes from a baby.

- You clean up any toilet mishap. **+6**
- You consider yourself the Prince of the Plunger. **+8**

- You've even got a holster −10
- it's monogrammed. −12
- But you're in therapy now. +3

- You clean up cat or dog (or any animal) excretion. +7
- You clean up vomit
- from a cat +8
- from a dog +10
- from a toddler +24 (sheer quantity raises points)
- from a local congressman. +45

- You chase a bat out of the house with a broom. +15
- You chase a small swarm of bees out of your backyard with a broom. +30
- You chase a Jehovah's Witness off your front porch with a broom. +35
- It's her mother. −35

- You get rid of a dead rodent. +12
- You get rid of a nest of crawling spiders. +13
- You remove Scruffy from the thresher. +30
- You take your mate's mother to see *Cats.* +45

··

THE AUTOMOBILE

You are not just the man of the house, but also king of the road. Which, as you'll see, doesn't really mean much of anything.

NAVIGATING SKILLS

- You leave the house for a distant destination, claiming you know exactly how to get there. **0**
- Thirty minutes later, you're lost. **−4**
- An hour has passed and you're still lost. **−8**
- You refuse to stop and ask for directions. **−10**
- And wherever you are doesn't look so safe. **−15**
- You finally decide to pull over and ask for directions. **0**
- You meet the locals up close and personal. **−20**
- She finds out you lied about having a black belt. **−60**

NAVIGATING SKILLS II

- A small furry animal darts into the road, and you do your best to avoid it. **+4**
- A small furry animal darts into the road, and you plow right over it **−5**
- and you cannot keep your inner satisfaction from bubbling over. **−40**
- You wait a few weeks before scrubbing the bumper. **−70**

NAVIGATING SKILLS III

- You tailgate. **−4**
- You don't let people merge. **−7**
- You yell at people who don't let you merge. **−9**
- You like to follow drivers who piss you off **−25**
- sometimes for miles and miles. **−75**
- Who cares if little Bobby has appendicitis! **−190**

CAR MAINTENANCE

- You always make sure the car's gas tank is brimming with unleaded. **+1**
- You make sure there are barely enough fumes to get the car rolling out of the driveway. **−1**
- But that's why you keep a siphon hose in the trunk. **−3**

IF YOU HIT IT, YOU LOSE

You're driving, and you hit:

- a parked car **−5**
- a moving car **−10**
- a tree **−15**
- a person **−20**
- an entire family **−30**
- a cat **−40**

DAY TO DAY DUTIES

You may have read about this in your local paper. Due to some undisclosed marital difficulties, a woman planned to kill her husband by rigging a primitive bomb in the washing machine. The strategy: the moment he would use the spin cycle, the machine would explode, sending him into the eternal tumble dry. Not only would this look accidental, his remains would be *bouncy fresh*.

Many in the press were horrified by this sick display of laundry terrorism. We, on the other hand, saw the upside to this. In order for the wife's plan to work, her mate must in fact *use* the washing machine. The moral: sharing the mundane chores of life is essential to the smooth running of our daily lives. Fulfill these duties and you achieve a domestic sainthood never realized by men who reuse dental floss or save their toenails to make crafts.

- You empty the trash nightly. **0**
- You empty the trash nightly, without being asked. **+1**
- You empty the trash only after the stench becomes unbearable. **–3**
- And when the raccoons are making themselves comfortable in the living room. **–10**

- You make the bed. **0**
- You make the bed, but forget to add the decorative pillows. **–1**
- You make the bed, add the decorative pillows, but neglect to fluff them. **–3**

- You put stuff away. **+2**
- You move stuff around. **+1**
- You move stuff around to make it look like you put stuff away. **–5**
- She trips over the chain saw in the living room. **–15**

- You leave the toilet seat up. **–1**
- You leave the toilet seat down. **0**
- You leave the toilet seat wet. **–3**
- There's a toilet seat? **–15**

- You replace the toilet-paper roll just before it runs out. **+2**
- You replace the toilet-paper roll when it's empty. **0**
- When the toilet-paper roll is empty, you resort to the box of Kleenex. **−1**
- When the Kleenex runs out, you use *People* magazine. **−4**
- When *People* magazine is gone, you shuffle slowly to the other bathroom. **−6**

- You empty the kitty litter box. **+2**
- You never empty the kitty litter box. **−5**
- You *use* the kitty litter box. **−15**

- When you come home from work, you neatly hang up your clothes in the closet. **0**
- When you come home from work, you remove your clothes, piece by piece, as you move from room to room **−2**
- and toss them on the floor **−5**
- except for the underwear, which you continue to wear another day. **−9**

- When you shave, you make sure always to clean up after yourself. **+1**
- When you're done shaving, you leave a coating of stubble in the sink **−3**
- and try out her Daisy shaver on "problem" areas. **−16**

- When you brush your teeth, you make sure to clean up afterward. **0**
- You leave milky paste all over the place. **−5**
- It dries, so you have to chip it off with a knife. **−6**
- You save the chunks to feed the cat. **−15**

- Every weekend, you straighten up the garage. **+5**
- Every weekend you plan on straightening up the garage, but you spend the entire time in a corner thumbing through your old *Playboys.* **–5**

- You sort the recyclables on a daily basis. **+1**
- You even rinse them out beforehand, so they won't attract bugs. **+3**
- You stack them neatly on the curb the night before pickup. **+1**
- You find yourself at 4:30 A.M. running out in your pajamas with the recyclables, just as the truck pulls away. **–5**
- So you leave them on the neighbor's lawn. **–7**

- You replace the smoke alarm batteries regularly. **+2**
- You then remove them whenever your Walkman runs down. **–5**

- When you dirty a dish, you rinse it and place it in the dishwasher. **+1**
- When you dirty a dish, you leave it in the sink on top of another dirty dish. **–1**
- When you dirty a dish, you rinse it off and put it back in the cupboard. **–5**
- When you dirty a dish, you let the dog's tongue do the scrubbing. **–45**

- When you dirty a dish you place it in the dishwasher **+1**
- without checking whether or not the dishes already in the dishwasher are actually dirty. **–5**
- They aren't. **–10**

- Per her request, you go out to buy her spring-fresh extra-light panty liners with wings. **+5**
- You return with a case of beer and a Black and Decker ⅝-inch power drill. **−15**

- You do the laundry **+3**
- but you don't separate **−4**
- you toss in your dirty underwear, her wedding dress, your jeans, and the living room curtains into the same cycle. **−15**
- The washing machine breaks free from the wall and leaves town for the weekend **−15**
- and her whites are now the color of faded denim **−9**
- but your jeans look great. **−10**

- You give the baby a bath **+10**
- with the garden hose. **−10**

- You vacuum regularly. **+6**
- You vacuum only after you've spilled something all over the floor while she's out of town **−4**
- like peanuts and chips **−6**
- or her grandma's ashes. **−140**

- You mop the floor, just to surprise her. **+10**
- You mop the floor, just so she won't be surprised. **−5**
- Who knew there was a top for the blender? **−35**

YOU CLEAN OUT YOUR:

- ears +**1**
- fingernails +**2**
- car +**5**
- retirement fund −**190**

....

KITCHEN HEROICS

Maybe you only visit the kitchen just to get to the fridge. Maybe you never even enter the kitchen, since you've moved the fridge to the bedroom. If that's so, you're missing out on a smorgasbord of points.

- You take an active part in the preparation of dinner. +**2**
- You're only trusted to boil water and/or remove food from the packaging −**5**
- and you still manage to use twelve pans −**15**
- and set off the smoke alarm. −**10**

- You use the oven on a regular basis +**5**
- but enough about drying your socks. −**17**

- You can actually cook a pretty decent meal. +**1**
- You can actually prepare two good meals +**2**
- macaroni and . . . cheese. −**12**

- You enjoy preparing risotto. +**10**
- You think risotto is the last name of a baseball announcer. −**10**

- You can make three great dishes using thyme. **+12**
- You can actually navigate a spice rack. **+15**
- You actually know Chef Boyardee's first name. **−30**

- The folks at the gourmet shop consider you a regular. **+8**
- So do the folks at the emergency room. **−20**

- You think you can make brownies. **+5**
- You think you can make it with a Brownie. **−25**

- You own an apron. **+5**
- You own an apron that has a humorous saying on it. **−4**
- "If the food sucks, then eat me." **−15**
- You wear it at picnics. **−20**
- Church picnics. **−25**

- You own a salad shooter. **+6**
- You've realized that it has many entertaining uses. **+10**
- Unfortunately, none of them have anything to do with food. **−23**

- You own a Cuisinart **+6**
- and you use it regularly **+7**
- to make cocktails. **−10**

- When throwing parties, you leave out snacks for guests. **+6**
- You offer "hits" from the Cheez Whiz cannister. **−6**

- You thought it would be nice to have your own ice cream maker **+2**
- so you go to the store and pick one up. **+3**
- Her name is Darlene. **−34**

REDECORATING

- You are highly knowledgeable about paint schemes. **+6**
- Enough to know the difference between burnt sienna and tattle teal. **+15**
- You always thought Dutch Boy was a kinky escort service. **–20**

- You've hung original contemporary works of art around the house. **+30**
- You've hung *posters* of contemporary works of art. **–30**
- You've hung beer company posters featuring big-busted women in tank tops. **–75**
- You tell your mate, "Hey, some day they'll be worth something!" **–100**

THE USES AND ABUSES OF TECHNOLOGY

Aside from vibrators, gadgets are strictly the stuff of men. But you'll find when dealing with any sort of gadgetry, there are inherent dangers involved. While we see them as high tech, she sees them as nothing more than toys. So handle with care. And always mail in the warranty.

ANSWERING MACHINE

- You have a very simple, direct message on your answering machine. **+1**

- You have a humorous message on your machine to express your creativity and wit. **−5**
- "Star Date 2051. We're not on the bridge right now . . ." **−30**

- You have cool music playing on your answering machine. **−2**
- "We will, we will ROCK you!!" **−20**
- And you do a lame morning zoo deejay voiceover. **−30**

COMPUTER

- You buy a computer with the expressed intent of organizing your family budget with it. **+5**
- Instead, you play DOOM **−15**
- and hang out in chat rooms pretending to be a twenty-one-year-old rock star in order to impress adolescent girls. **−30**
- When your mate asks you why the family budget hasn't been organized, you plead carpal tunnel syndrome. **−60**

THE VCR

- You know how to program the VCR **0**
- so it will tape her favorite show when she's not home to watch it. **+4**
- You accidentally tape over one of her favorite shows **−5**
- with an episode of "Baywatch." **−6**
- Okay, it wasn't an accident. **−8**

- When your mate is home alone, she decides to pop in the video (*Beaches*) she picked up on the way home from work. **0**
- You forgot to remove one of *your* movies in the machine. **−15**
- She watches, and can't help but notice how much *larger* those "actors" are. **−40**

- You tape all the important shows she likes. **+3**
- You never label them. **−6**
- It takes two frightening hours to find that "special" tape both of you made when you were drunk. **−34**
- You accidentally returned it to Blockbuster. **−70**

THE REMOTE CONTROL

- You buy a brand new universal remote, but not because the old one was broken **0**
- but because the new one comes with a holster **−5**
- and the buttons on the old remote were worn down. **−8**

THE CAR PHONE

- You buy a cellular phone for her car, just so she can get in touch with you in case of an emergency, and vice versa. **+15**
- You use it to gauge how long it will be before she gets home from wherever she is. **−15**
- "You'll be home in about twenty minutes? Uh, that's all, can't wait to see you!" **−45**
- And she still catches you wearing her dresses. **−450**

CHAPTER SUMMARY:
WHAT HAVE WE LEARNED?

- Even though it sounds like one, a deep throat socket is not a plaything.
- Never use her curling iron to unclog a toilet. Try her hairbrush. Works like a charm.

- Weekend projects rack up points. Especially if you hurt yourself in the process. Try to preserve your limbs, however.
- Learn to embrace vomit, toilet troubles, and roadkill. It will be the only time she'll love you despite the way you smell.
- It may be your car, but it's her domain. Forget that rule, and you'll never enjoy her plush interior. Get rid of the scented tree freshener.
- Simple things like emptying the trash and changing the oil take little effort, but will keep you in good graces. Ignore them, and three months from now you'll be living in a studio apartment above a dive bar eating soup from a can.
- Which is one more reason to learn how to cook.

....

THE SCORECARD GIFT SHOP

Here's what you get for what you did.

- Paint the den = an afternoon watching football at home.
- Paint the den + the color of her choice = an afternoon watching football + at Hooters
- Clean a dead skunk off the driveway + deposit it in the woods a mile down the road = a beer with a single pal + at a sports bar.
- Clean a dead skunk off the driveway + deposit it in the woods a mile down the road + return with freshly picked wildflowers = Poker Night!
- Put together a piece of furniture = two tall beers + a big bag of Doritos.
- Put together a piece of furniture + you injure yourself while doing it = four beers + a big bag of Doritos + one trip to the emergency room.

PERSONAL HABITS AND MORE (OR LESS)

When you lived alone, you could walk around naked, eat dinner naked, watch television naked, sleep fully clothed. Things are different now. All those little habits you thought were harmless now carry significant point values. And worse, the points just don't add up when you're home. She's keeping score wherever you are.

....

THE PIG FACTOR

A man's gotta do what a man's gotta do. But it will cost you.

- belching **–4**
- farting **–8**
- either, in public **–12**
- both, in bed **–16**

- You wear clean underwear every day. **0**
- You wear clean underwear when you remember to change them. **–10**

- Your underwear has more skidmarks than the Indianapolis Speedway. **–20**

- You shave daily, even on the weekends. **+1**
- You don't shave on the weekends. **–1**
- On the other hand, neither does she. **+1**

- You shower daily. **0**
- You shower only when you think you "need" it. **–20**
- You shower only when you need to wash your clothes. **–50**

- You shower after your evening workout. **+1**
- You never shower after your workouts. **–5**
- When she says you stink, you reply that you think you smell "earthy." **–20**

You use the shower for certain practices other than bathing, such as:
- sex **+9**
- sex, by yourself **–15**
- while she's drying her hair. **–45**

- You clean out your belly button regularly. **+1**
- You've been saving the lint. **–23**
- You're looking forward to unveiling your float at the upcoming parade. **–80**

- You talk on the phone while in the bathroom. **–10**
- To an all-sports radio talk show. **–25**

- You trim your nails. **+5**
- You trim your nails in the living room **–10**

- using your teeth −**15**
- and flicking the trimmings at the cat. −**20**

- You flush the toilet when you're finished. **0**
- Still, you always leave a little something behind. −**5**

- You have a drink now and then. **0**
- You're a regular at a bar. −**20**
- It's a cozy place where "everyone knows your name." −**40**
- Because you're the guy who threw up on the dance floor. −**80**

YOUR RAMPANT USE OF THE HIGH FIVE

- You high five after an exceptional sports play. −**3**
- You high five after a good meal. −**15**
- You high five after good sex. −**100**
- You high five after a really good high five. −**120**

FAST WAYS TO LOSE POINTS

From simple throwaway glances to meaningless comments you say without thinking—they may seem like small change to you. But to her they're a cash cow. Moo.

- whistling −**1**
- singing −**1**
- performing show tunes at breakfast −**34**

- laughing loudly –1
- snickering sinisterly –1
- guffawing without a care –2
- chuckling with abandon –2
- being mean to squirrels –5

- playing air guitar –2
- playing air guitar and bobbing your head up and down –3
- at a religious service –8

- chugging beer –4
- chugging whiskey –44
- at breakfast –270

- flicking beer bottle caps at the television –4
- flicking beer bottle caps at her –9

- telling a dirty joke –4
- telling a dirty joke she doesn't understand –13

- looking at someone else –5
- who looks back –15
- from a passing school bus –45

- yawning –2
- yawning while she's talking –4
- yawning while she's crying –14

- doing a crossword puzzle –1
- filling it with swear words –12
- in French –37

- reading the classifieds to look for a job –**3**
- but peruse the personals instead. –**14**

- checking yourself out in a mirror –**4**
- checking yourself out in a car window –**6**
- checking yourself out of rehab –**25**

- snapping your fingers to a really bad song –**2**
- snapping your fingers to absolute silence –**5**
- snapping your fingers to country music –**45**

- tossing an object from one place to another –**5**
- like dirty laundry –**6**
- wadded up paper –**7**
- a small child –**35**

- trying to make out the naked people on the scrambled Playboy Channel –**4**
- trying to remove the clothes off a lingerie catalog using an eraser –**25**

WHEN YOU COME HOME SMELLING LIKE:

- too much cologne –**5**
- alcohol –**10**
- cigarettes –**20**
- Chanel No. 5 –**150**
- German shepards –**250**
- gunpowder –**270**
- Richard Simmons –**400**

- picking your nose –5
- picking your ears –4
- picking a small piece of food from your teeth –4
- looking at it and eating it –10

- picking anything from your pubic hair –40
- and showing it to her –50

- smelling your clothes –4
- smelling your pits –6
- smelling your farts –16

- smoking cigarettes –16
- smoking a pipe (and you're under fifty-five) –15
- smoking a crack pipe –20
- and you're not a Hollywood celebrity –490

- tossing peanuts in the air and catching them with your mouth –6
- tossing grapes in the air and catching them in your mouth –12
- tossing anything in the air and catching it with your butt –45

LOATHSOME BEHAVIOR

- sniveling –25
- pleading –50
- whining –75
- carefree self-confidence –100

- cracking your knuckles –**2**
- cracking your back –**4**
- cracking a safe –**145**

- squeezing a pimple –**3**
- asking her to squeeze your pimple –**9**
- asking her nicely to squeeze your pimple –**14**

- counting your blessings +**4**
- counting your change –**4**

- living with your mother –**56**
- in a trailer park –**89**
- and lying about it –**100**

YOUR WEAKNESSES

- She catches you looking at a woman—just for a second. –**10**
- You're caught looking again a few minutes later. –**14**
- Same woman. –**21**
- Different woman. –**30**
- She's not a woman. –**39**

- measuring your penis –**6**
- naming your penis –**10**
- making a shadow puppet with your penis –**7**
- and you're so pleased by this you're thinking of putting on a show –**112**

- urinating in her aquarium **–20**
- because it's closer than the bathroom **–45**

- wrestling playfully with her **–6**
- and breaking something expensive **–15**
- like, say, her clavicle **–90**

- talking in a funny voice because you think it's amusing **–8**
- the voice sounds remarkably like her mother's **–8**

- taking a self-help test in one of her magazines **+6**
- and flunking **–6**
- then changing your answers **–12**
- you still flunk **–24**

- reading her diary **–123**
- out loud to your friends **–200**
- in a funny voice **–275**

- You relieve yourself with the bathroom door shut. **0**
- You relieve yourself with the bathroom door ajar. **–5**
- You relieve yourself in the fountain at Rockefeller Center. **–45**

- You use her bath towel and you don't put it back. **–5**
- You use it to dry below the waist. **–8**
- You do the back-and-forth routine between your thighs. **–22**

- You get up before she does. **+2**
- You get up later than she does most of the time. **–7**
- When she leaves for work, you're still in bed. **–18**

- When she comes home from work, you're out of bed **0**
- because you've moved to the couch. **−45**

- You roll your eyes whenever she says something. **−2**
- You roll your eyes and say "here we go again," whenever she says something **−7**
- like, "I'm pregnant." **−45**

You do all of this in front of her friends **−14**
- or *your* friends **−21**
- while driving her to the emergency room. **−45**

- You whistle in the supermarket. **−3**
- You whistle loud enough to be heard from across the frozen food section. **−6**
- You whistle Black Sabbath's "Ironman" loud enough to be heard from across the entire store. **−12**
- You start attracting groupies. **−25**

STUFF SHE FINDS IN YOUR POCKETS

- a love poem you wrote about her **+20**
- a love poem you wrote about yourself **−30**

- a ring, meant as a surprise **+50**
- the surprise is, it's not for her **−150**

- a condom **+3**
- and she's on the pill **−60**

- a key to a hotel room **0**
- a key to a room at a hotel she doesn't recall staying at **–45**
- well, at least with you **0**

- a crumpled receipt **0**
- for dinner at an expensive restaurant **0**
- that she wasn't at **–45**
- and someone ordered veal **–135**

- two plane tickets for a trip you said nothing to her about **–432**
- along with a copy of the floor plans of a nearby bank **–570**
- and two tickets to *La Cage Aux Folles* **-600**

- You hum or tap your toes when waiting for something:
- an elevator **–2**
- a traffic light to turn green **–2**
- for her to get out of the bathroom **–5**
- for her to give birth to your child. **–90**

- You play air guitar when a classic AC/DC song comes on. **–7**
- You play air guitar when a classic AC/DC song comes on, in the presence of company. **–14**
- You play air guitar when a classic AC/DC song comes on while driving. **–18**
- You actually believe there's such a thing as a classic AC/DC song. **-24**

- You glance at the television—if even for a brief second—to check out the sports highlights, while she's talking to you. **–10**
- You glance at the television—if even for a brief second—to check out the sports highlights, while you're making love. **–35**
- You change positions to get a better view of the fourth quarter drive. **–76**

STUFF YOU LEAVE AROUND THE HOUSE

- You leave cups and dishes in the bedroom. **–3**
- You leave clothing in the living room. **–5**
- You leave bath towels on the bathroom floor. **–7**
- You leave a blond wig, eyeliner, and red pumps in your bottom drawer. **–15**

YOUR PHYSICAL HEALTH AND WELL-BEING

When you get out of shape, you become a constant and highly visible reminder that you no longer care about appearing attractive to her. As a result, she will stop caring, too. Pretty soon both of you will be poster children for SlimFast.

- You weigh exactly the same amount that you weighed when you first met her. **+2**
- You were really fat back then. **–4**

- You have actually lost weight since the first time that you met her +5
- because you never make it home for dinner. −15

- You have actually gained weight since the first time you met her. −10
- You're on Richard Simmons' speed dial. −200

- You lost the weight because you work out vigorously and pay attention to what you eat. +15
- You lost weight because of a particularly active tapeworm −10
- and you've kind of warmed up to the little bugger. −30

- Since you have been with her, you have developed a rather large potbelly. −15
- You have developed a large potbelly, and you've started running to get rid of it. +10
- You have developed a large potbelly, and resort to loose-fit jeans and baggy, wide Hawaiian shirts to get rid of it. −5
- Actually, you have given your potbelly a nickname. −10
- "The Big Guy." −11
- You let the neighbor kids bounce on it. −23
- When you're not selling advertising space on it. −45

- You go to the gym every morning before you get to work. +15
- You try to make it to the gym three times a week, at lunchtime during work. +3
- You head to Jim's every night after work for pitchers of beer and wings. −35

- You have a personal trainer. **+5**
- You've "had" your personal trainer. **−45**

- You have rippling biceps **+10**
- covered by rippling fat. **−10**

- You have a powerful set of pectoral muscles **+12**
- made of plaster, in your steamer trunk. **−12**
- Your real chest is sunk deeper than the *Andrea Doria*. **−20**

- You have what's known as a "six-pack." **+25**
- You have absolutely no abdominal muscles to speak of **−15**
- due to what's known as a "six-pack."**−30**

- You have muscular, well-defined legs. **+10**
- You have pudgy, penguin-like legs. **−10**
- You haven't seen your legs in three years. **−45**

- You look good naked. **+20**
- You look respectable in boxers and a tank top. **0**
- Your neighbors keep leaving you curtains on your front porch. **−65**

YOUR DIET REGIMEN

- You always read the labels of the foods you buy, and make sure every item you purchase is either a reduced-fat or low-fat product. **+15**
- And now you eat twice as much food as you did before. **−30**

- You use nonfat cooking spray instead of butter. **+4**
- You use herbs instead of salt **+3**
- and your Big Mac tastes better than ever. **−15**

- You don't use sugar on your morning cereal. **+2**
- You find that breaking up candy bars over your Froot Loops is far tastier. **−4**

- You admire the dietary restraint of the vegetarians you know. **+1**
- You admire the dietary restraint of Idi Amin. **−45**

- You gave up using fattening condiments like mayonnaise on your sandwiches. **+2**
- You find it much more appealing to eat it straight from the jar. **−23**

- When you dine at restaurants you always order the "healthy heart" meal. **+4**
- Because you love to eat "healthy hearts." **−55**

- When dining out you ask that butter and oil not be used in the preparation of your meal **+5**
- and that the salad dressing be served on the side **+2**
- then you order the chocolate cheesecake **−13**
- and you wonder why the waiters spit in your food. **−15**

THE MORE POUNDS YOU GAIN, THE MORE POINTS YOU LOSE

- You're ten pounds overweight. **–5**
- You're twenty-five pounds overweight. **–40**
- You can no longer squeeze in behind the steering wheel of your car. **–190**

YOUR PLANS FOR THE FUTURE

- You quit your job without talking to her first **–50**
- and remain jobless for months. **–75**
- You get really fat. **–175**
- You end up sitting around watching daytime talk shows. **–400**
- You end up appearing on daytime talk shows **–500**
- with your new drag queen boyfriend. **–700**
- It's Dennis Rodman. **–1400**

FINANCES

- You spend a lot of money on something impractical. **–10**
- You spend a lot of money on something impractical that even she can't use. **–20**
- Such as a motorized model airplane **–25**

- or an elaborate train set you plan on setting up in the basement **−40**
- or one of those midget cars Shriners drive in parades. **−50**
- Meanwhile, your kids need braces **−60**
- in fact, all four of them do. **−120**

- You make a lot of money **+4**
- and save none of it. **−10**
- You invest it wisely. **+5**
- Actually, you've made some really dumb investments. **−25**
- Like the O. J. Simpson Sleepaway Camp. **−140**
- You still think it's going to take off. **−250**

- You like to put your money in mutual funds. **+25**
- You like to put your money into those brown penny wrappers. **−65**

- You get excited when the stock market hits new highs. **+5**
- You get excited when you find coins under the couch cushions. **−10**

HOW YOU SCORE WHEN YOU'RE BETTER THAN HER AT:

- board games **−3**
- driving **−4**
- sports **−5**

- finances −**6**
- laundry −**10**
- cleaning −**15**
- cooking −**20**
- expressing yourself −**24**
- dealing with her parents −**25**
- dealing with your kids −**30**
- breastfeeding −**60**

DINING MATTERS

- You eat potato chips out of a bowl. **+1**
- You eat potato chips out of a bag. −**1**
- You eat chips out of the crevice between the armrest and cushions of your couch. −**15**

- You eat stuff that comes out of a can. −**3**
- You eat stuff *in* the can. −**45**

WHENEVER YOU EAT OUT OF:

- a bag −**2**
- a box −**4**
- a pants pocket −**10**
- a dumpster −**30**

- You always use plates and the proper utensils. **+1**
- Every container spout is perfectly contoured to your lower lip. **−13**
- Including the Crisco. **−45**

- You eat standing over the kitchen sink **−5**
- at Denny's. **−15**

- You talk with your mouth full **−4**
- and the eulogy still ran over by an hour. **−59**

- In the morning you prepare for both of you a complete, healthy breakfast, with cereal, toast, juice, fresh strawberries, and skim milk. **+4**
- In the morning, you reheat last night's leftovers **−15**
- which are still in a red and white cardboard bucket. **−30**

Around the house, you snack on:
- fresh fruit and cut vegetables **+5**
- chips and candy **−8**
- whatever's floating in the aquarium. **−35**

HOW TO HANDLE FINGER FOODS

Women know where we put our fingers. That's why it will cost you when you use your digits to devour:

- hot dogs **0**
- chili **−6**
- spaghetti **−15**
- paste **−40**

CHAPTER SUMMARY:
WHAT HAVE WE LEARNED?

- Women don't like stepping on your clipped fingernails when they're walking barefoot. So buy them slippers.
- Suck in your gut at all times. Even when sleeping.
- It has had a long and happy life, so please let the high five die once and for all.
- Spaghetti is not a finger food, as much as you'd like it to be. But ravioli—well, that's another story altogether.

THE SCORECARD GIFT SHOP

Here's what you get for what you did.

- You shave daily = so does she.
- She catches you drinking out of a carton = you clean the kitchen.
- She catches you playing air guitar + making the "guitar solo" face = you rake the lawn + make the "raking the lawn" face.
- You lose twenty pounds = she loses ten pounds.

9

SPORTS, RECREATION, FIREARMS, AND OTHER ASSORTED AMUSEMENTS

Sure, it's all fun and games—until you realize who's really keeping score.

....

PLAYING GAMES

TENNIS

- When you play tennis with your mate, you prefer to let her keep score. **+2**
- When you play tennis with your mate, you prefer to keep score. **−2**
- You keep score accurately. **−5**
- You announce the score regularly **−7**
- and you've found that Mr. Microphone really seems to help. **−52**

- When you play, you take the game seriously. **−8**
- When she hits a ball out, you call it out. **−5**

- When her serve is long, you say it's long. −5
- You argue over close calls. −12
- You argue over every call. −17
- You do all of this during the practice volley. −25

- When you play tennis, you keep score −3
- but you make sure she's always ahead +4
- until the end, when you crush her like a fly. −74

- She brags to her friends how she's beaten you ten times this month +40
- and she's not talking about tennis. 0

- You win at tennis handily, and give her game tips along the way. −20
- You tell her she's holding the racquet improperly −25
- and that she doesn't throw the ball high enough for her serve −25
- or that she'd volley better if she opened her eyes −20
- or dropped a few pounds. −80

- When you win a game, you act modest. 0
- You have your own special victory dance. −34

- You actually hate playing tennis with your mate. −5
- You do it just to make her happy +5
- and to get high from sniffing the new can of tennis balls. −10

GOLF

- You play golf. −15
- She doesn't play golf. −20

- You play golf regularly. −**45**
- You belong to a golf club. −**50**
- You live on a golf course. −**60**
- At parties you stand around and work on your grip with an imaginary club −**70**
- while wearing really embarrassing plaid knickers. −**150**

- You watch golf on television. −**15**
- You read golf magazines. −**20**
- You correspond with Fuzzy Zoeller. −**40**

- You keep your golf gear out of the house in the garage. +**5**
- Tees keep clogging up the washing machine. −**135**

- You used to love golf, but you gave it up because of her. +**16**
- She uses your golf bag as a planter just to rub it in. +**25**

- When playing golf together, you forgo the rules +**4**
- which means you let her throw the ball instead of chipping it. +**7**
- Whenever her first drive stinks, you let her try again. +**2**
- Whenever her second drive stinks, you let her try again. +**3**
- You find yourself saying, "Don't worry dear. Three holes in five hours is plenty for me." +**9**

- When she has a short putt, you call it a "gimme." +**5**
- You do this whenever she's about to tee off, too. +**15**

BOWLING

- You don't bowl. **+5**
- You bowl occasionally. **−4**
- You belong to a bowling league. **−40**
- You've got a "jacket." **−50**

SOFTBALL LEAGUE

- You belong to a softball league. **−14**
- You don't belong to a softball league. **+1**
- You belong to a softball league because you actually enjoy the game **−5**
- and the free beer **−10**
- and the snug uniforms **−15**
- and it beats going home right after work. **−25**

....

HOBBIES AND OTHER LEISURELY PURSUITS

Yours will never matter as much as hers. Your mission: accompany her on her dreaded escapades, and pretend to like it. And realize that whatever hobby you hold dear will always cost you points.

- When she goes to a flower show, she goes alone. **0**
- You go with her. **+2**
- You pretend to enjoy it. **+4**
- When she forces you to sit through lectures about watering procedures for the daffodil, you sit quietly and smile **+4**
- and nod at appropriate times. **+6**
- Soon, it becomes clear you've been drinking **−24**

- especially when you display your own "watering" procedures for the daffodil. **−76**

- You accompany her shopping for antiques. **+4**
- The little shops are dusty and musty, and run by cranky old women. **+5**
- Your mate spends freely, buying stuff you wouldn't even keep in your garage **+9**
- which you lug out in boxes to the car. **+4**
- and then stack with the rest of the "antiques" **+3**
- which still are in boxes in the garage **+12**
- next to your "collection" of pristine *Playboys*. **−12**

- You like to play poker. **−5**
- You like the stuff you get to do while playing poker **−7**
- like drinking beer **−8**
- like smoking cheap cigars **−11**
- like swearing a blue streak **−13**
- and losing all of the grocery money. **−33**

HOBBIES THAT COST YOU POINTS

- collecting German Hummel figurines **−8**
- collecting German au pairs **−65**
- building a model train city in the basement **−11**
- and hold tours **−40**
- playing golf **−18**
- playing miniature golf **−36**
- developing an herb garden in your bathtub **−19**

- developing a strange fascination with the films featuring the Gabor sisters. **–25**
- calling into sports radio talk shows **–100**
- acting in community theater **–150**
- but only musicals **–300**

SPORTING EVENTS

The irresistible combination of tangy ballpark franks, the roar of the crowd, and getting frisked by a husky woman at the entrance all add up to a singularly wonderful experience. But this whole dynamic changes once you bring your mate. The strategy: make sure you're on your best behavior. So ditch the Styrofoam finger, will ya?

BASEBALL

- You get two great seats in the reserved section right behind third base. **+5**
- You get two mediocre seats somewhere behind home plate. **+1**
- You get a bench in left field, up in the nosebleed section. **–6**
- You're sharing the bench with a rowdy group of glue sniffers. **–11**
- You tell her it's to save money for beer. **–15**

- A line drive is hit in your area, and you dive across three rows to catch it. **–6**

- You catch it. **+4**
- You keep the ball. **−5**
- You hand it to your mate. **+10**
- You give it to a young boy sitting nearby. **+15**
- You trade it for his wheelchair. **−150**

- During the seventh-inning stretch you stand up and put your arm around her and sing "Take Me out to the Ballgame." **+2**
- You sing it poorly. **−2**
- You sound okay. **+2**
- You drunkenly collapse on the family below you **−10**
- which is broadcast on the giant scoreboard **−25**
- and replayed on the local news. **−50**

FOOTBALL

- You arrive at the stadium a few hours early to barbecue hamburgers and hot dogs and eat a lot of tasty homemade potato salad. **+5**
- You arrive at the stadium a few hours early to drink lots of cheap beer in the parking lot **−10**
- and urinate behind parked cars **−15**
- while singing "We are the Champions." **−20**

- You bring a nice wool blanket to cover you and your mate when the temperature drops. **+5**
- You left the blanket at home because you couldn't fit it in the car. **−15**
- Those enormous "We're Number 1!" signs you painted on refrigerator boxes took up all the room. **−45**

- You root enthusiastically for your team, without using profanity or offending anyone nearby. **+5**

- You strip down and belly bump with another half-naked guy. −23
- You invite him back later for post-game Yahtzee. −55

....

WATCHING TELEVISED FOOTBALL

Nothing is more troublesome than watching pro football with your mate. This is in part because women, more or less, are repulsed by any activity in which a person can be penalized for holding someone.

You choose to watch a football game, when you could be:
- mowing the lawn −4
- sorting out the family finances −8
- painting the den −10
- attending her mother's funeral −160

- You are watching a football game −3
- with your mate −2
- with your mate in a hotel room, in Paris, France. −356

- When your team scores, you display mild pleasure. 0
- You show more pleasure than during sex −15
- not that she remembers. −34

- When the other team scores you display mild displeasure. 0
- You jump up and down and wave your hands wildly −15
- as the car veers into a duck pond. −145

- You invite your mate to watch the game with you. +3
- You explain the intricacies of the game to her. +3

- You don't mind when she interrupts you with questions during the game. **+3**
- You explain that it's just padding in their pants. **−4**

- You have a bunch of loudmouth friends over to watch the game. **−5**
- You let her watch the game with you and your friends. **+1**
- They enact instant replays using her "antiques." **−25**
- They fumble on third and long. **−45**

WHAT YOU EAT WHILE WATCHING A GAME

- brie and crackers, and a nice Merlot **+4**
- low-fat chips and nonfat salsa **+3**
- expensive microbrewed beer **0**
- any food that changes the color of your fingers **−5**
- a pig rotating on a large spit in the driveway **−30**

CHAPTER SUMMARY: WHAT HAVE WE LEARNED?

- Let your mate win at everything. That includes Parcheesi, thumbwrestling, and marital counseling.
- Your hobbies mean nothing. Her hobbies mean everything. So find something the both of you can do together. And then don't do it.
- Never explain the rules of football to your mate. Women should look at football the same way we look at feminine hygiene products. It's better left a mystery.

THE SCORECARD GIFT SHOP

Here's what you get for what you do.

- You let her win at tennis = beer and burgers afterward.
- You cream her at tennis = you fend for yourself.
- You spend Saturday playing golf with your pals = you spend Sunday at her parents.
- You have your friends over to watch football – they leave peanut shells and beer cans all over the house = you become well acquainted with your local florist.

10 SNEAKY WAYS TO SCORE POINTS

Now, not all of us are born into wealth. And not all of us are terribly good looking. This puts us at a disadvantage when we want to impress women. Worse, guys who do have all the material goods and high cheekbones tend to score points easier than the rest of us, and that forces women to reserve their wrath for the rest of us.

So we need to even up the playing field, so to speak.

No problem. There are some exceedingly simple (dare I say, devious?) ways to earn points, none of which will cost you a dime. And best of all, they are completely legal in most states and U.S. territories (with the exception of Guam).

It's called lying.

When you want to create a mysterious yet alluring past:

- you occasionally drop hints about a profound experience that occurred in your childhood **+4**
- you insist that you really don't want to talk about it, because you're so modest **+6**
- and you were obviously deeply affected by this experience **+8**

- enough not to hold down a job for no longer than six months. **−33**

- But if she presses you, you'll break down and tell her the story. **+6**
- But you swear she mustn't tell anyone. **+11**
- That makes her feel really special. **+12**
- Your eyes water as you tell her that many years ago you rescued a woman from a well **+15**
- actually it was Mother Teresa. **+30**
- your mate wonders why Mother Teresa would be stuck in a well in Scranton, PA. **−45**
- You tell her she was thirsty. **−100**

When you want to appear as though you have a cool past:

- you casually mention the name of somebody famous that you once dated **+10**
- you casually mention the name of somebody famous that you dumped because she became too possessive. **+30**
- you "accidentally" leave a fabricated love letter out in the open, written by that person. **+45**
- the letter is signed, "Love, Uma." **+60**
- the letter is signed, "Love, RuPaul." **−220**

When you want her to think you're a really sensitive guy:

- you pay a friend she doesn't know to leave messages on your answering machine that portray you in a highly favorable light, and you let her overhear them **+5**
- "We greatly appreciate your substantial contribution to the 'Save the Poor, Indigent, Starving Children Fund.'" **+7**
- "Your book of poetry for the oppressed will be published in the spring." **+15**

- "The president is concerned you have not returned his calls."
  +20
- "Hey, this is Sting. Are we still on for Friday night?" **+25**

You want her to think you lead an exciting, daring life.

- You casually mention that you are in the CIA. **+10**
- Right now you are involved in a highly sensitive situation. **+12**
- It involves major espionage work in the U.S.S.R. **+20**
- She mentions that the U.S.S.R. doesn't exist anymore. **−40**
- You say, "Ah . . . or so they'd like to have you think." **+10**

You want to cultivate the idea that you lead a really, really cool life.

- You tell her you're in a band. **+10**
- You're the lead singer. **+20**
- You tell her the band has just been signed to a major label. **+25**
- But you turned down the offer, because it violates your artistic integrity. **+40**
- But working at Starbucks for minimum wage doesn't. **−20**

You want her to believe that she is a big priority.

- You turn down imaginary but extremely important work functions or parties, in order to spend more time with her. **+10**
- You turn down phony invitations from attractive women in order to be with her. **+15**
- You call in sick from work to be with her. **+25**
- You're a pediatric neurosurgeon **−30**

You want her to think you're well-rounded.

- You mention that you have lived abroad for many years. **+5**

- You mention that you have lived with many broads in one year. **−45**

- You mention that you lived among aborigines in Newfoundland. **+22**
- She says there are no aborigines in Newfoundland. **−22**
- You say, "I know. Isn't that the ultimate tragedy?" **+13**

You want her to think you're going places.

- You have a screenplay "in the works." **+20**
- You've gotten a few major "bites." **+30**
- You've fielded calls from "Mel," "Bruce," and "Al." **+35**
- But you're holding out until Brando loses weight **+55**
- because, "He owes me one. " **+60**

You want her to think you're athletic.

- You talk about your days as a tennis player at Harvard **+1**
- or as a basketball player at UCLA **+7**
- or as quarterback for Nebraska. **+15**
- or, more truthfully, as a male cheerleader at Chico State. **−60**
- "Would you like to see the uniform?" **−80**

When you want to seem like a jock, you bring out:

- your old football helmet **+4**
- your old baseball glove **+5**
- your old jock **−30**

You want her to believe that you are very desirable.

- You pay a woman to proposition you in front of your mate. **+15**
- You pay this woman to cry when you flatly turn her down. **+25**
- You tell your mate that's why you stopped dating royalty. **+60**

You need to garner sympathy.

- You fake a rare illness. **+30**
- You tell her you have only a few months to live **+139**
- unless you partake in a very special experimental treatment. **+30**
- It involves repeated applications of fellatio. **–30**

You need to be seen as a hero.

- You pay a few friends to stage a mugging. **+12**
- You defend your mate against these "ruthless thugs" **+15**
- with some very keen karate moves. **+50**
- She recognizes one of the guys from your bowling league. **–130**

You want her to believe you're very sensitive.

- You sometimes mention your "inner demons." **+5**
- You wear a beret. **+6**
- You carry around a well-thumbed copy of Proust. **+7**
- You break down crying at odd times **+10**
- until the manager at Starbucks tells you to get back to work. **–23**

- You write her a love poem **+25**
- which she recognizes from *The Norton Anthology of Poetry*. **–25**
- You say, "Oh, so you've read my work." **+30**

- You often talk about your time spent in the Vietnam War. **+30**
- You refer to it as 'Nam. **+70**
- You're only twenty-seven. **–70**

11 SUCCEEDING WITH THE SCORECARD

By now, you've acquired a better understanding of the mechanics of the female mind. The question now, of course, is how to use this new-found expertise. Below we offer you some skill-building exercises to help improve upon your already formidable talents. Just remember, use these skills only for good, not evil. But first . . .

THE LIFE SPAN OF YOUR BAD DEEDS

Whether you break an arm, cut yourself shaving, or ruin your reputation with a homemade porn movie, you incur some kind of damage. And with any damage, you must expect a certain amount of time for the ugly wounds to heal properly.

The same rule applies when you screw up in love.

Thankfully, The Scorecard makes it easy to estimate how long you will be in the doghouse, given your point deficit. By quantifying your bad deeds, you make it fairly simple for yourself to calculate your coming parole. Here's how it breaks down:

Point Values vs. Estimated healing time

- **one point** = one minute, or until she becomes preoccupied with something else. Change her mind quickly by doing something nice. And we don't mean telling her she looks sexy when she's mad.
- **five points** = four hours, give or take three days. Again, act quickly, and you can minimize the chance of inflammation. We suggest flowers. By the way, it won't work giving her the money you'd spend on flowers.
- **15 points** = one to two days, punctuated with silent glares. You might want to lay low for a while (look into the availability of the spare bedroom or the back of a flatbed truck).
- **30 points** = three days. But it will feel like one long, long week. Do not expect sex. At least with her. Pick up after yourself, and look reasonably clean, and she may remember why she likes you. If she doesn't, wave your paycheck in front of her. It works like smelling salts.
- **50 points** = five days. By that time, she should get tired of being mad at you. If not, then you might start fixing anything you've been meaning to fix in the past six months. And we're not referring to the dog.
- **100 points** = one to two weeks. It may take longer, depending on whether your actions also caused grave financial damage, or ruined the carpeting. Sever all ties with anyone involved in your foolish actions—and that includes the Pope.
- **200 points** = three weeks to one month. Settle in for a long spell. Your only strategy: try not to bring up ugly memories of whatever you did that angered her so. That means severing ties with the girl's field hockey team.
- **1000 points** = one year, or more. By then, we're counting on her completely forgetting—or accepting—the things you did

that pissed her off. If she hasn't, settle in for a long, hellish life, punctuated by visits from her parents and many hours arranging potpourri.

ALLTIME POINT LOSERS

- chronic unemployment **–100**
- chronic weight gain **–200**
- chronic belching, farting, nose-picking **–250**
- sleeping with members of her immediate family **–1500**
- suggesting breast implants **–500**
- armed robbery **–750**
- taking up golf **–760**
- agreeing with her mother when they're arguing **–2000**

ALLTIME POINT GAINERS

- not missing a single Lamaze class **+300**
- delivering the baby yourself **+400**
- in an elevator **+450**
- in a grain elevator **+555**

- letting her name the baby after a dear relative from her side of the family **+100**
- a relative that you cannot stand **+200**
- named Eunice **+200**

- making lots of money **+2000**
- spending it all on her **+3000**

- bankrolling her second career (the more useless this vocation is, the more points you earn)
- portrait painting **+1000**
- pottery-making **+1200**
- law school **+2000**

- bailing her brother out of jail **+200**
- for the third time **+400**

- taking her on a very expensive vacation **+300**
- flying first class all the way even though you can't afford to **+400**
- staying at only five-star hotels even though you can't afford to **+400**
- taking her parents along **+500**
- you even leave your golf clubs behind **+600**

···

15 QUESTIONS: A QUIZ

The military never sends its pilots out on real death-defying missions without first putting them through hours and hours in flight simulators. The same rule applies here. Below are a series of sensitive questions aimed at gauging your Scorecard expertise. Call it a *relationship-simulator*.

1. *The ideal way to mention your mate's weight problem is:*

   A. to talk to her about it openly and honestly
   B. to leave cans of SlimFast around the house

C. there is no ideal way to mention your mate's weight problem

Answer: C. If you answered A or B, you are already headed for trouble. And this is just the first question. Might we suggest a snack break?

2. When your mate argues with her mother in front of you, you should:

A. help resolve the issue at hand by pointing out the value of both of their points of view
B. pick sides, depending on who's preparing dinner that night
C. hide in the basement

Answer: C. This is just a safety precaution. Only choose B if you haven't had lunch.

3. Given the choice to either work late to earn more money for her, or come home to spend more time with her, you should:

A. work late to earn more money
B. come home and spend time with her, even if it means not making as much money.
C. do one or the other, because really it doesn't matter

Answer: C. You are going to get heat for A or B. If you work late, she'll think you're neglecting the relationship. If you don't work late, she will question your ambition. There is one antidote, however: bring work home with you. She'll still complain that you're ignoring her, but at least you'll look responsible while doing it.

4. If you and her decide to live together, you should:

    A. let her move in with you

    B. move in with her

    C. move in, but keep your old place across town—*just in case*

    D. find a larger place together to call home

Answer: B. By moving in with her, you immediately discard about 90 percent of your furniture, which she hated to begin with. You do, however, get to keep your electric shaver. As for C, only rich people and senators from Massachusetts get to do that.

5. When meeting one of her friends, you should always:

    A. be polite and engage in conversation

    B. bring up her skin condition

    C. wear a muscle shirt and not say anything

Answer: C. No matter how careful you are, A will lead to B in most circumstances. Your best bet: shut up and flex.

6. The first thing you should do every morning is:

    A. Get up and make coffee for both of you

    B. make love

    C. brush your teeth

    D. go downstairs, warm up her car

    E. masturbate

Answer: A, followed by C, followed by D. They must all be done in that sequence, and then you may be eligible for B. If not, you'll have to plan on E for the time being. Just don't do it in front of her.

7. *When you play a game of tennis, you should:*

   A. let her win
   B. wear really nice clothes
   C. lose the silly headband

Answer: A, B, and as a precaution: C.

8. *When you go bowling, you should*

   A. let her win
   B. not go bowling

Answer: B. Most women find any sport or activity that requires them to put on pre-worn shoes they don't own to be extremely repulsive.

9. *When she tries on an outfit and asks you for your opinion, you:*

   A. say it looks fine
   B. tell her it makes her look heavy
   C. say, "I thought the other one showed off your figure"
   D. give her the credit card and excuse yourself to the men's room

Answer: D. This is what's known as an escape maneuver.

10. *Before making love with your partner, you should always:*

   A. dim the lights
   B. remove your clothing.
   C. remove her clothing.
   D. ask the guests to leave.

Answer: D. It's only polite.

11. *When an old girlfriend calls, you:*

    A. pretend it's a wrong number and hang up

    B. pretend it's a wrong number and hang up, then call back when your mate isn't around.

    C. tell her that you're involved with someone, and you'd appreciate it if she would stop calling you at home

    D. then add "So call me at work"

    E. ask her what she's wearing

Answer: C. That way, you avoid trouble and buy some time to entertain various sexual fantasies that will never come to pass in real life. And of course, you will not call her back. Right? Right?

12. *When your mate wants to have a serious conversation, you:*

    A. listen intently, with a concerned expression

    B. tell her you'd love listen, but you believe the room is bugged

    C. hand her the Magic Eightball, which you purchased for such an occasion

Answer: A. Like you have a choice?

13. *When she spends a lot of money on something impractical or worthless (like, say, a bread machine) you:*

    A. say nothing, and walk quietly away

    B. try to persuade her that the item should be returned

    C. go out and do the same thing, spending a lot of money on something just as impractical (like, say, another bread machine)

Answer: A. Whenever she buys anything, accept it. This is how capitalist economies work. If women did not go out and purchase ridiculous appliances without our prior knowledge, then this great country of ours would collapse (see Russia).

14. *She wants to go to the mall. You want to watch the game. You suggest:*

- A. a compromise. She goes to the mall, and you stay home and watch the game
- B. a compromise. She goes to the mall, and you drop her off—then leave to watch the game at a sports bar. And you pick her up on the way home.
- C. a compromise. You go with her to the mall, and go to every store with her, and miss the game entirely.

Answer: C. It may not sound like a compromise to you, but that's what it is to her. She gets to shop, and you get to spend time *with her* while she shops. And that, in her opinion, should make both parties very happy. Agreed?

15. *She asks you: Have you forgotten what today is? You reply:*

- A. "Oh . . . it's . . . uh . . . *that* day, right?"
- B. "No, I haven't forgotten. I was just waiting to see if *you* had forgotten."
- C. "No, I haven't. Just let me go out and get the gift. It's in my car. I'll be right back." And you drive off slowly so she doesn't here the tires screech.
- D. "I believe it's a Canadian holiday."

Answer: B. This clever strategy allows you to bounce the question back to her. Of course, this doesn't work if it's actually her birthday. Which, given the odds, it probably is.

Scoring

15 *out of* 15: Excellent! Your understanding of romance is impressive. No doubt, that will be of great benefit if you're ever incarcerated!

10 or more out of 15: Good job. But you can do better. Stop playing poker in the nude.

Less than 10: You've got a long way to go. Consider therapy. Or better, more hair care products.

12 YOUR NUMBER IS UP

Congratulations. You've reached the end of this great journey through the bizarre and intricate world of the female psyche. And, we hope, without having to purchase tricolor pasta.

By now, you should have learned many things. One is exactly how women judge male behavior, and another is how important it is to keep lap dancing charges from appearing on your credit card. But more important, you have made a new friend. The Scorecard. Keep it close by, and you will always have what it takes to make a woman happy. And by doing that, you will gain a certain measure of happiness for yourself. Plus, you'll get to have sex with the lights on. At the museum, no less.

See, as you become more and more adept at pleasing your mate, you'll build up a vast point fortune and gain a level of freedom only known to rock stars and investment bankers. And then you can do just about anything (provided it doesn't involve automatic weapons or parties at Kelsey Grammer's house).

As you follow this book's advice however, you will experience one particular side effect. Your friends, neighbors, and concerned strangers will look at you differently. They will stare.

They might even run from you—screaming. Far worse, they may even try to check your basement for extraterrestrial pods.

Don't be alarmed. These folks are simply scared of what they don't understand. For you, dear friend, have become a different kind of man. A man who is not only sensitive to the needs of women, but a man who has willingly allowed all masculine thoughts and deeds to be drained from his blood. That is harsh stuff, my friend, but it is a small price to pay to bring joy to the fairer sex. Now get on with your servitude. And don't forget to pick up the dry cleaning. That's three points!